Your Turn
Practice Book

 Education

Bothell, WA • Chicago, IL • Columbus, OH • New York, NY

P9-DHM-893

www.mheonline.com/readingwonders

The McGraw·Hill Companies

 Education

Copyright © The McGraw-Hill Companies, Inc.

All rights reserved. No part of this publication may be
reproduced or distributed in any form or by any means, or
stored in a database or retrieval system, without the prior
written consent of The McGraw-Hill Companies, Inc.,
including, but not limited to, network storage or
transmission, or broadcast for distance learning.

Send all inquiries to:
McGraw-Hill Education
2 Penn Plaza
New York, NY 10121

Printed in the United States of America.

7 8 9 RHR 17 16 15 14

Contents

Unit 1 • Friends and Family

Copyright © The McGraw-Hill Companies, Inc.

Contents

Unit 2 • Animal Discoveries

Copyright © The McGraw-Hill Companies, Inc.

Contents

Unit 3 • Live and Learn

Copyright © The McGraw-Hill Companies, Inc.

Contents

Unit 4 • Our Life/Our World

Copyright © The McGraw-Hill Companies, Inc.

Contents

Unit 5 • Let's Make a Difference

Copyright © The McGraw-Hill Companies, Inc.

Contents

Unit 6 • How on Earth?

Copyright © The McGraw-Hill Companies, Inc.

Name _____

actions	afraid	depend	nervously
peered	perfectly	rescue	secret

Use what you know about the words in the sentences to choose the word that makes sense in each blank. Then write the word on the line.

1. The boy can _____ on his friend to help him.

2. She _____ into the dark room.

3. The man helped _____ people from danger.

4. The friends sang the song together _____ in tune.

5. The girl was not _____ to try something new.

6. Do not tell anyone the _____.

7. The mouse looked around _____ for the cat.

8. We watched the soccer players' quick _____.

Copyright © The McGraw-Hill Companies, Inc.

Name _____

Listen to each short vowel sound as you say the words
pan and _fit_.

**A. Say the name of each picture. Circle the word that has
the same vowel sound as the picture name. Write the
word on the line.**

1. six   fun   _____

2. lot   wag   _____

The endings -_s_ or -_es_ make nouns mean more than one.

B. Read each word. Write the base word.

3. mats _____   4. bags _____

5. kisses _____   6. fans _____

Copyright © The McGraw-Hill Companies, Inc.

Name _____

> To figure out a new word, separate the **root word** from the ending. The endings *-s, -es,* and *-ing* mean the action is happening now. The ending *-ed* means the action happened in the past.

A. Read each sentence. Look at each underlined word. Draw a line between the root word and the ending.

1. Van's eyes <u>opened</u> wide.

2. Food booths were set up <u>showing</u> colorful flags.

3. People were <u>selling</u> Greek salad there.

B. Underline the verb in each sentence. Then change each verb so that it tells about action happening now. Write the new word.

4. Mom stopped at the first booth.

   _____

5. At last, the family reached the end of the street.

   _____

Copyright © The McGraw-Hill Companies, Inc.

Name _____

Reread "The Food Festival." Write about how the author used details to develop realistic characters and events in the story.

1. In "The Food Festival," the characters are _____

_____

_____.

2. The author included details, such as _____

_____

_____ to make the characters seem realistic.

3. Story events, such as _____

_____

_____

are realistic because _____

_____

_____.

4. The author included these events to show _____

_____

_____.

Copyright © The McGraw-Hill Companies, Inc.

Name _____

decide	different	friendship	glance
proper	relationship	stares	trade

A. Read each clue below. Then find the vocabulary word on the right that matches the clue. Draw a line from the clue to the word.

1. look at quickly   **a.** proper

2. not the same   **b.** friendship

3. correct   **c.** decide

4. looks at for a long time   **d.** trade

5. make up your mind   **e.** glance

6. being pals   **f.** different

7. give one thing for another   **g.** relationship

8. a connection with someone   **h.** stares

B. Choose one vocabulary word from the box above. Write the word in a sentence of your own.

9. _____

_____

Copyright © The McGraw-Hill Companies, Inc.

Name _____

Two letters can be blended together, such as **cl, dr, sk, sl,** and **st.** Listen to the beginning sounds in **slip** and the ending sounds in **best.**

A. Look at the picture. Write the missing blend for each word.

1.  _____ ick   2.  ma _____

3.  _____ ock   4.  _____ ed

5. 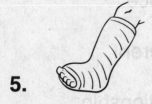 ca _____   6.  _____ ess

When two consonants come between two vowels, you divide the word between the two consonants to find the syllables.

B. Divide each word into syllables. Write the syllables on the lines provided.

7. velvet _____ _____   8. contest _____ _____

9. picnic _____ _____   10. sudden _____ _____

Copyright © The McGraw-Hill Companies, Inc.

Name _____

Read the passage. Ask and answer questions as you read to check your understanding.

A Pet of His Own

Jeff lived with his family and their three pets. His
10 sister Kim had a bird. His brother Rick had two mice.
21 Jeff wanted a pet of his own. "May I get a snake?" he
34 asked his parents. He was polite because he knew good
44 manners were important.

47 "A snake will eat my bird," shrieked Kim loudly. Her
57 yell upset her bird. The bird started to chirp.

66 Jeff had another idea. "May I get a cat?" he asked
77 politely.

78 "A cat will eat my bird," cried Kim.

86 "And a cat will eat my mice," said Rick.

Copyright © The McGraw-Hill Companies, Inc.

Name _____

95   Jeff was stumped by his pet problem and didn't know
105 how to solve it. He wanted a pet that was different and
117 unique. There was already one bird and two mice. He
127 couldn't get a snake or a cat. What kind of pet wouldn't
139 disturb or upset the others?

144   Then one day Jeff saw an ad for a rabbit. This pet was
157 different. This pet could get along with the others.

166   Jeff's parents got him the rabbit. He was so thrilled to
177 have a pet of his own that he shouted for joy.

Copyright © The McGraw-Hill Companies, Inc.

Name _____

A. Read the draft model. Use the questions that follow the draft to help you use more precise words.

Draft Model

My kitten is a good size for my family's small apartment. She can sleep on my lap. She has nice fur. My kitten likes to be outside and so do I.

I. What size is the kitten?

2. What color is the kitten's fur? How does it feel?

3. What does the kitten like to do outside?

B. Now revise the draft by replacing general words with more precise, interesting words about the kitten.

_____

_____

_____

_____

_____

_____

Copyright © The McGraw-Hill Companies, Inc.

Name _____

The Perfect Reading Partner

Reading was not easy for Lizzie.
One day, her cat Gumbo jumped
in her lap while she was reading.
Lizzie read aloud to Gumbo.
She did not make one mistake.
Gumbo was a great listener!

Answer the questions about the text.

1. How can you tell that this text is fiction?

_____

_____

2. What happens at the beginning of the story?

_____

3. What happens in the middle?

_____

4. What happens at the end?

_____

Copyright © The McGraw-Hill Companies, Inc.

Name _____

> Look at this example of **context clues**. The underlined words explain what *polite* means.
>
> He was **polite** because he knew <u>good manners were important</u>.

Read each sentence. Then circle the meaning of the word in bold print that makes sense. Underline the context clues.

1. "A snake will eat my bird," **shrieked** Kim <u>loudly</u>.

   (yelled)   whispered

2. Jeff was **stumped** by his pet problem and <u>didn't know how to solve it</u>.

   happy   (confused)

3. He wanted a pet that was <u>different</u> and **unique**.

   the same   (not like others)

4. What kind of pet wouldn't **disturb** or <u>upset the others</u>?

   (bother)   enjoy

5. He was so **thrilled** to have a pet of his own that <u>he shouted for joy</u>.

   angry   (excited)

Copyright © The McGraw-Hill Companies, Inc.

Name _____

Reread "A Pet of His Own." Write about how the author used character, setting, events. Use the words and picture to complete the sentences.

1. In the beginning of the story, the author tells us that the main

   character _____

   _____

   _____ .

2. In the middle of the story, _____

   _____

   _____ .

3. At the end of the story, _____

   _____

   _____ .

4. The author organized the events in this order to show _____

   _____

   _____ .

Copyright © The McGraw-Hill Companies, Inc.

Name _____

| allowed | care | excited | needs |
| roam | safe | wandered | wild |

Choose the word that makes sense in each blank. Then write the word on the line.

1. An animal living in the _____ is different than a pet.

2. Dogs are not _____ in the park.

3. A cat that has _____ from its yard might get lost.

4. The girl takes good _____ of her pet hamster.

5. The children were _____ about getting a new pet.

6. A pet's _____ include water, food, and exercise.

7. Our cat keeps her kittens _____ from danger.

8. Pets live with people, but animals in the jungle _____ free.

Copyright © The McGraw-Hill Companies, Inc.

Short a, Long a (a_e)/Inflectional Endings -ed, -ing

Name _____

The letter **a** can stand for the short **a** sound you hear in **can**.
The long **a** sound you hear in **cane** can be spelled **a_e**.

A. Circle one short a word and one long a word in each sentence. Write each word in the correct list below.

1. The ducks swam in the lake.

2. We wave to the man on the bus.

short a   **long a**

3. _____ 5. _____

4. _____ 6. _____

The ending **-ing** can be added to a verb to show that an action is happening right now. The ending **-ed** can be added to a verb to show action that has already happened.

B. Add -ed and -ing to the end of each word. Write the two new words.

7. fix   _____ _____

8. pack   _____ _____

9. play   _____ _____

10. lock   _____ _____

32 Practice • Grade 2 • Unit 1 • Week 4

Name _____

Read the passage. Ask and answer questions as you read to check your understanding.

A Fire Dog

     Wilshire is a fire dog. He lives in the city. When

11 Wilshire first came to the fire station, he was just three

22 months old. He lived at the fire station day and night.

33 Fifty firefighters lived and worked there, too. They took

42 care of Wilshire. They fed the young dog. They gave

52 him water to drink.

56   The firefighters hired a dog trainer. The trainer gave

65 Wilshire lessons. He helped Wilshire learn to live in the

75 fire station. He showed Wilshire where he could go. He

85 showed Wilshire where he was not allowed to go.

94   Then it was time for exercise. Wilshire didn't even

103 have to go outside. He was trained to run on a treadmill

115 inside the station.

Copyright © The McGraw-Hill Companies, Inc.

Name _____

Fire dogs like Wilshire are often a breed called Dalmatians.

118   Soon Wilshire became close pals with one firefighter.
126 Now Wilshire and the firefighter spend a shift at the
136 fire station together. Then the firefighter takes Wilshire
144 home. This gives Wilshire a break from the busy station.
154 He also has fun meeting and playing with other dogs.

164   Wilshire got even more training. Now he can do fire
174 safety tricks. He visits schools and shows children how
183 to "Stop, Drop, and Roll." All that work keeps Wilshire
193 very busy!

John Connell/Corbis

Copyright © The McGraw-Hill Companies, Inc.

Name _____

A. Reread the passage and answer the questions.

I. How did the firefighters take care of Wilshire?

_____

_____

2. Why did the firefighter take Wilshire home?

_____

_____

3. What does a Dalmatian look like?

_____

_____

B. Work with a partner. Read the passage aloud. Pay attention to how your voice rises and falls as you speak naturally. Stop after one minute. Fill out the chart.

	Words Read	–	Number of Errors	=	Words Correct Score
First Read		–		=	
Second Read		–		=	

Copyright © The McGraw-Hill Companies, Inc.

Name _____

Read the selection. Complete the Key Details chart.

Detail	Detail	Detail

Copyright © The McGraw-Hill Companies, Inc.

Name _____

A. Read the draft model. Use the questions that follow the draft to help you think about how to use sequence words.

Draft Model

Here's how to give a dog a bath. Fill the tub with warm water. Get the dog in the tub and wash her with soap. Rinse her with plenty of fresh water. Dry the dog with a towel.

---

1. To give a dog a bath, what do you do first?

2. What do you do next? Then what?

3. What is the last thing you do?

B. Now revise the draft by adding sequence words such as *first, next, then,* and *last* to help readers understand the order of ideas.

_____

_____

_____

_____

_____

_____

Copyright © The McGraw-Hill Companies, Inc.

Name _____

The Foster Pet

Amy's family has a foster pet. They feed and play with Rocky and take him to the vet. They train him to follow commands. When Rocky gets bigger, another family will give him a lasting home.

Amy trains Rocky to walk on a leash.

Answer the questions about the selection.

1. How can you tell this text is a nonfiction narrative?

_____

_____

2. What is one way that Amy trains Rocky? How did you find this information?

_____

_____

3. What does the text help you learn about a foster pet?

_____

_____

Juice Images/age fotostock

Copyright © The McGraw-Hill Companies, Inc.

Name _____

> To figure out a new word, separate the **root word** from the ending. The endings *-s, -es,* and *-ing* mean the action is happening now. The ending *-ed* means the action happened in the past.

Read each sentence. Look at each underlined word. Draw a line between the root word and the ending. Then write the meaning of the word.

1. He <u>lives</u> in the city.

   _____

2. Fifty firefighters lived and <u>worked</u> there, too

   _____

3. He <u>helped</u> Wilshire learn to live in the fire station.

   _____

4. Then the firefighter <u>takes</u> Wilshire home.

   _____

5. He also has fun <u>meeting</u> and playing with other dogs.

   _____

Copyright © The McGraw-Hill Companies, Inc.

Name _____

Reread "A Fire Dog." Think about how the author used key details. Use the words and photo to complete the sentences.

I. This selection is about _____

_____

_____.

2. The author includes details about _____

_____

_____.

3. The photo shows _____

_____

_____.

4. The details and picture help me understand _____

_____

_____.

Copyright © The McGraw-Hill Companies, Inc.

Name _____

checks	choose	chores	cost
customers	jobs	spend	tools

**A. Choose the word that makes sense for each clue.
Write the word on the line.**

1. pay money to buy something _____

2. looks at something closely to make sure it is okay _____

3. people who buy things _____

4. equipment used to make or fix things _____

5. small jobs around the house _____

6. how much you have to pay for something _____

7. work people do to earn money _____

8. to decide on one thing rather than another _____

**B. Choose one vocabulary word from the box above.
Write the word in a sentence of your own.**

9. _____

_____

Copyright © The McGraw-Hill Companies, Inc.

Name _____

> The letter *i* can stand for the short *i* sound you hear in *fit*. The long *i* sound you hear in *fine* can be spelled *i_e*.

A. Read each word. Circle the words with the short *i* sound. Underline the words with the long *i* sound.

> pipe   did   tip   five   hike   fin   side   pick

> A possessive noun ends with an apostrophe (') and an *s* to show who owns something.

B. Rewrite each phrase using a possessive noun.

1. the kite that belongs to the girl

_____

2. the job that belongs to Mom

_____

3. the dish that belongs to the cat

_____

4. the ball that belongs to the dog

_____

Copyright © The McGraw-Hill Companies, Inc.

Name _____

Read the passage. Ask and answer questions as you read to check your understanding.

Family Business

Families may start up a business. The family
08   members all pitch in to make it work. Then the business
19   is passed down through the family. Here's one family
28   business that has been around for 95 years.

36   In 1916, two families started a new business. They
45   opened a coffee company. They roasted the coffee beans
54   by hand. There were no cars then. They used horses and
65   wagons to deliver the coffee.

70   The coffee business grew. More family members came
78   to work for the company. In 1918, the company was able
89   to buy its first truck.

Copyright © The McGraw-Hill Companies, Inc.

Name _____

Family Business Then and Now

1916	Today
Roasted coffee beans by hand. Delivered coffee using a horse and wagon.	Sell coffee in stores, restaurants, and online. Make ads for TV.

94   In the 1940s, sons of the owners joined the business.
104 The company grew. It sold coffee to restaurants. The
113 company soon needed a bigger office.

119   By the 1990s, the third generation was working for the
129 company. The company started selling its coffee in new
138 places. They sold coffee food stores. They made ads for
148 TV. In 2007, they opened an online store.

156   These family members worked hard. They made their
164 business a success. Now they can pass it on to the next
176 generation.

Copyright © The McGraw-Hill Companies, Inc.

Name _____

A. Reread the passage and answer the questions.

1. What happened in 1916?

_____

_____

2. What happened in the 1940s?

_____

_____

3. What happened in 2007?

_____

_____

B. Work with a partner. Read the passage aloud. Pay attention to how you pause and group words together. Stop after one minute. Fill out the chart.

	Words Read	–	Number of Errors	=	Words Correct Score
First Read		–		=	
Second Read		–		=	

Copyright © The McGraw-Hill Companies, Inc.

Name _____

Read the selection. Complete the Key Details chart.

Detail	Detail	Detail

Copyright © The McGraw-Hill Companies, Inc.

Name _____

A. Read the draft model. Use the questions that follow the draft to help you think about using sentences of different types and lengths.

> ### Draft Model
>
> I like to help my family get chores done. It makes our house clean. It also gives us free time together. That's what I love best.

1. Where could you add a question?

2. Where could you add an exclamation?

3. Which sentences could you make longer? Which sentences could you make shorter?

B. Now revise the draft by writing some questions or exclamations and by writing some long sentences and some short sentences.

_____

_____

_____

_____

_____

Copyright © The McGraw-Hill Companies, Inc.

Name _____

Family Pizza Shop

Some families own a pizza shop. Everyone helps out.
The adults make the food and help customers. The kids
can help clean tables and windows after school.

Adults' Jobs	Kids' Jobs
make food	clean tables
help customers	clean windows

Answer the questions about the text.

1. How can you tell this is an informational text?

_____

_____

2. What does the chart show?

_____

_____

3. What are the adults' jobs in a pizza shop?

_____

_____

Copyright © The McGraw-Hill Companies, Inc.

Name _____

To figure out new words, look at word parts. A root word may have the ending **-s, -es,** or **-ed**. The endings -s and -es mean a noun is plural. The ending -ed means an action happened in the past.

Read each sentence. Circle the ending of the underlined word. Use what you know about root words and endings to write the meaning of each underlined word.

1. <u>Families</u> may start up a business.

   _____

2. Here's one family business that has been around for 95 <u>years</u>.

   _____

3. In 1916, two families <u>started</u> a new business.

   _____

4. In the 1940s, sons of the owners <u>joined</u> the business.

   _____

5. It sold coffee to <u>restaurants</u>.

   _____

Copyright © The McGraw-Hill Companies, Inc.

Name _____

Reread "Family Business." Write about how the author uses key details. Use the words and chart to complete the sentences.

I. In "Family Business," one key detail that the author includes is

_____

_____ .

2. Another key detail that the author includes is _____

_____

_____ .

3. The author includes a chart that shows _____

_____

_____ .

4. It helps me understand _____

_____

_____ .

Copyright © The McGraw-Hill Companies, Inc.

Name _____

| adapt | climate | eager | freedom |
| fresh | sense | shadows | silence |

Use what you know about the words in the sentences to choose the word that makes sense in each blank. Then write the word on the line.

1. My sister is excited and _____ to learn about polar bears.

2. The quiet _____ ended when birds began to chirp.

3. Desert animals must _____ to hot, dry weather.

4. The air feels cool in the dark _____ under the trees.

5. The eagle has the _____ to fly where it wants.

6. A rainforest has a warm, wet _____.

7. The air outside felt _____ and clean.

8. A wild animal will run away if it feels a _____ of danger.

Copyright © The McGraw-Hill Companies, Inc.

Name _____

> The letter **o** can stand for the short **o** sound you hear in **not**.
> The long **o** sound you hear in **note** can be spelled **o_e**.

A. Read each word. Circle the words with the short o sound. Underline the words with the long o sound.

> box   nose   rope   lock   pot   cone   dog   home

> Before adding **-ed** or **-ing** to some verbs with short vowels, double the final consonant. Before adding **-ed** or **-ing** to some verbs with long vowels ending in e, drop the final e.

B. Add -ed and -ing to the end of each verb. Write the two new words.

1. save   _____   _____

2. trip   _____   _____

3. hug   _____   _____

4. joke   _____   _____

Copyright © The McGraw-Hill Companies, Inc.

Name _____

**Read the passage. Use the make predictions strategy
to predict what will happen in the story.**

Looking for Animals

   Ms. Lee takes her class to the woods for a hike. She
12 tells her students to look for woodland animals. All the
22 children carry notebooks. They plan to sketch and take
31 notes about the animals they will see.

38   The group sets off down the path. High above, birds
48 sing in the trees. One boy points to what he thinks is a
61 robin. The others disagree. They say it is just a leaf.

72   The children hear hooting. It is unlike the other
81 sounds. They look up but are unable to see anything.
91 An owl looks down at them. Its brown feathers blend in
102 with the leaves. The children can not see the owl.

Copyright © The McGraw-Hill Companies, Inc.

Name _____

112   The children pass by a small pond. A deer is drinking
123 there, but it stands still as the group walks by. Its brown
135 coat makes it seem to disappear into the woods. The
145 deer slips away unseen.

149   One girl looks down at the uneven path. She sees
159 what look like small lumps of dirt. Then she stops
169 watching. The lumps jump away. No one has seen the
179 tiny toads that blend in with the ground.

187   The hike is over. The class retraces their steps back to
198 the bus. The driver unlocks the door. Maybe the class
208 can return another day to look for more animals!

Copyright © The McGraw-Hill Companies, Inc.

Name _____

A. Reread the passage and answer the questions.

1. What happened at the beginning of the story?

_____

_____

2. What happened in the middle of the story?

_____

_____

3. What happened at the end of the story?

_____

_____

B. Work with a partner. Read the passage aloud. Pay attention to where you pause as you read. Stop after one minute. Fill out the chart.

	Words Read	–	Number of Errors	=	Words Correct Score
First Read		–		=	
Second Read		–		=	

Copyright © The McGraw-Hill Companies, Inc.

Name _____

Read the selection. Complete the Character, Setting, Plot chart.

Character

Setting

Plot

Copyright © The McGraw-Hill Companies, Inc.

Name _____

A. Read the draft model. Use the questions that follow the draft to help you add descriptive details.

Draft Model

Meg and Tom go to the beach. They swim in the water. Meg sees birds flying in the sky. Tom finds shells on the beach. Then they see a crab near the water!

I. What kind of beach is this? What kind of day is it?

2. What details can tell more about the birds, shells, and crab that Meg and Tom see?

3. What details might tell how Meg and Tom feel about their day at the beach?

B. Now revise the draft by adding descriptive details that help readers learn more about the setting and characters.

_____

_____

_____

_____

Copyright © The McGraw-Hill Companies, Inc.

Name _____

Surviving the Winter

In the summer, Jerry saw a family of chipmunks in his yard. What would they do in the cold winter? Jerry looked up chipmunk habits and learned they would hibernate all winter.

Answer the questions about the text.

1. How do you know this text is realistic fiction?

_____

_____

2. How does Jerry find out information about chipmunk habits?

_____

_____

3. How does Jerry know the chipmunks will survive the cold winter?

_____

_____

Copyright © The McGraw-Hill Companies, Inc.

Name _____

> To figure out a new word, look for a **prefix**, or word part at the beginning of the word.
>
> The prefix *re-* means "again."
>
> The prefix *un-* means "not."
>
> The prefix *dis-* means "opposite of."

Read each sentence. Underline the word that has a prefix. Then write the word and its meaning.

1. The others disagree.

   _____

2. They look up but are unable to see anything.

   _____

3. Its brown coat makes it seem to disappear into the woods.

   _____

4. The deer slips away unseen.

   _____

5. The class retraces their steps back to the bus.

   _____

Copyright © The McGraw-Hill Companies, Inc.

Name _____

Reread "Looking for Animals." Think about how the author used details to support the genre of the story. Use the words and picture to complete the sentences.

I. The story is realistic fiction because the author wrote about

_____

_____.

2. I know it is realistic fiction because the characters _____

_____

_____.

3. The author included realistic events such as _____

_____

_____

to help support the genre.

Copyright © The McGraw-Hill Companies, Inc.

Name _____

| believe | delicious | feast | fond |
| lessons | remarkable | snatch | stories |

Read the story. Choose words from the box to complete the sentences. Then write the answers on the lines.

There are some _____ that teach

_____. This is one of those tales. Lion was

very _____ of cherries. He said, "I

_____ that cherries are the best food!"

When Lion heard that Hippo had lots of

_____ food, he went over to take a look.

Seeing all of Hippos's food made him want to

_____. On the table was a bowl of the biggest

cherries he had ever seen. "That's _____!"

thought Lion. He made a plan to _____ the

cherries. Then he ran home with them. At home, Lion

bit into a cherry. They were wax! The cherries had not

been worth taking after all.

Copyright © The McGraw-Hill Companies, Inc.

Name _____

> The letter *u* can stand for the short *u* sound you hear in *cut*.
> The long *u* sound you hear in *cute* can be spelled *u_e*.

A. Choose the word from the box that names each picture. Write it on the line.

> mule   tub   cub   flute

1. _____

2. _____

3. _____

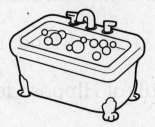

4. _____

> Vowel consonant *e* syllables often have the long sound of the vowel.

B. Divide each word into syllables. Write each syllable.

5. pancake _____ _____

6. excuse _____ _____

Copyright © The McGraw-Hill Companies, Inc.

Name _____

Read the passage. Use the make predictions strategy to predict what will happen in the story.

Fox Gets Help

One day, Fox was walking in the woods. High in a
11 tree, he saw a nice bunch of grapes. "Those will make a
23 healthful snack," Fox thought. He jumped up to get the
33 grapes. ·

34   Fox nearly reached the grapes, but he could not jump
44 high enough. He really wanted those grapes. So Fox
53 made a plan. He got a ladder and leaned it on the tree.
66 He should be able to reach the grapes easily.

Copyright © The McGraw-Hill Companies, Inc.

Name _____

75   The wind began blowing strongly. As Fox stepped up
84 to the ladder, the wind blew it down on the ground. This
96 happened over and over again. Fox sighed loudly. He
105 was about to give up. Then Turtle crept up slowly.

115   Turtle had an idea that was helpful. He would hold
125 the ladder tightly while Fox climbed up. Fox went up the
136 ladder and picked the bunch of grapes.

143   When Fox was safely back on the ground, he shared
153 the grapes with Turtle. Fox was thankful for his friend's
163 help. Sometimes it takes a friend to help you reach a
174 goal.

Copyright © The McGraw-Hill Companies, Inc.

Name _____

A. Reread the passage and answer the questions.

1. What was the problem in the story?

_____

_____

2. What steps did Fox take to solve the problem?

_____

_____

3. What was Fox's solution to the problem?

_____

_____

B. Work with a partner. Read the passage aloud. Pay attention to expression. Stop after one minute. Fill out the chart.

Copyright © The McGraw-Hill Companies, Inc.

	Words Read	–	Number of Errors	=	Words Correct Score
First Read		–		=	
Second Read		–		=	

Name _____

Read the selection. Complete the Problem and Solution chart.

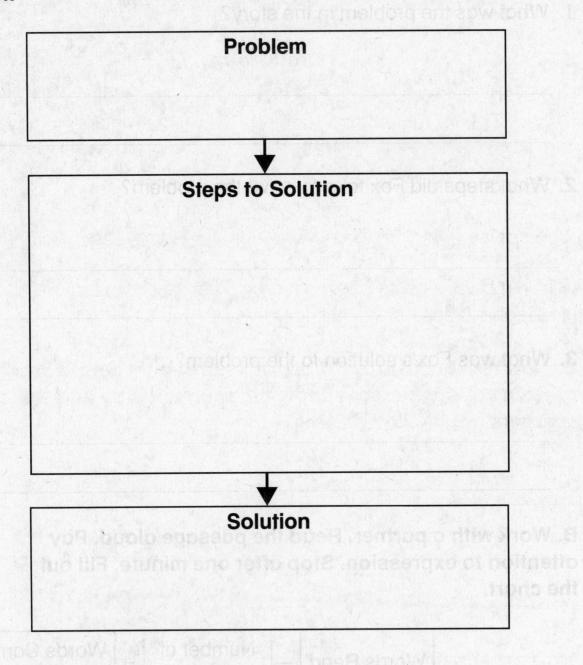

Problem

↓

Steps to Solution

↓

Solution

Copyright © The McGraw-Hill Companies, Inc.

Name _____

A. Read the draft model. Use the questions that follow the draft to help you add supporting details.

> **Draft Model**
>
> Every day a shepherd boy thought he saw a wolf. "Wolf!" he cried. The villagers came running. They felt sorry for the boy.

1. How does the shepherd boy feel?

2. What is he thinking about when he thinks he sees a wolf?

3. What details could explain more about the actions of the shepherd boy and the villagers?

B. Now revise the draft by adding supporting details that explain your ideas about how the shepherd boy and the villagers act, think, and feel.

_____

_____

_____

_____

_____

Copyright © The McGraw-Hill Companies, Inc.

Name _____

The Fox and the Grapes

One day the fox saw a bunch of grapes high in a tree. He could not reach the grapes. The fox walked away. "Those grapes must be sour," he said. It is easy to dislike something you cannot get.

Answer the questions about the text.

1. How can you tell that this text is a fable?

_____

_____

2. What happens at the beginning of the fable?

_____

_____

3. What happens at the end of the fable?

_____

_____

4. What lesson does the fable teach?

_____

Copyright © The McGraw-Hill Companies, Inc.

Name _____

| buried | escape | habitat | journey |
| nature | peeks | restless | spies |

A. Read each clue below. Then find the vocabulary word on the right that matches the clue. Draw a line from the clue to the word.

1. the outdoor world   **a.** habitat

2. takes a quick look   **b.** escape

3. the natural place where an animal lives   **c.** spies

                                                      d. buried

4. get away

                                                      e. peeks

5. cannot stay still

                                                      f. nature

6. a long trip

                                                     g. journey

7. covered up in the ground

                                                     h. restless

8. watches and sees something

B. Choose one vocabulary word from the box above. Write the word in a sentence of your own.

9. _____

_____

Copyright © The McGraw-Hill Companies, Inc.

Name _____

> The **c** in ***cent*** stands for the /s/ sound. It is soft **c**. The **g** in ***germ*** stands for the /j/ sound. It is soft **g**.

A. Read each word in the box. Then write the words that belong in each list.

> space   range   trace   cage   badge   ice

Soft *g*	Soft *c*
I. _____	4. _____
2. _____	5. _____
3. _____	6. _____

> A **prefix** is a word part added to the beginning of a word to make a new word.
> - The prefix ***re-*** means "again."
> - The prefixes ***un-*** and ***dis-*** mean "not" or "opposite of."

B. Read each word. Write its meaning.

7. dislike _____   8. reuse _____

9. unkind _____   10. redo _____

Copyright © The McGraw-Hill Companies, Inc.

Name _____

Read the passage. Use the make predictions strategy to predict what you will learn.

Two Kinds of Tundra

The Arctic Tundra

3   Dr. Jones went to the **Arctic tundra**. It was very cold
14 with no trees. There were grasses and flowers. Dr. Jones
24 was hopeful that he would see animals. He made a
34 careful study of what he found.

40   In the sky, Dr. Jones saw playful **ravens** and **gulls**.
50 On the ground, he saw **gray wolves** and **Arctic**
59 **hares**. He knew that many of these animals had extra
69 fat. This was useful. It kept the animals warm during
79 the cold winter. Some of the animals slept while others
89 went south.

Copyright © The McGraw-Hill Companies, Inc.

Name _____

91 **The Alpine Tundra**

94   The next trip Dr. Jones took was to the **alpine**
104 **tundra**. He was greatly interested in comparing the two
113 places. This tundra did not have trees, either. The alpine
123 plants were almost like the Arctic plants. The animals
132 were clearly different, though.

136   Dr. Jones saw birds such as **jays** and **grouse**. He saw
147 **sheep** and **elk**. He knew that some of these animals
157 also had extra fat. It kept them warm. Some of these
168 animals slept through the winter. Others went south.

Brand X Pictures/Getty Images

Copyright © The McGraw-Hill Companies, Inc.

Name _____

A. Reread the passage and answer the questions.

1. What is the main topic of the passage?

_____

_____

2. What is a key detail about the Arctic tundra?

_____

_____

3. What is a key detail about the alpine tundra?

_____

_____

B. Work with a partner. Read the passage aloud. Pay attention to how you group words together as you read. Stop after one minute. Fill out the chart.

	Words Read	–	Number of Errors	=	Words Correct Score
First Read		–		=	
Second Read		–		=	

Copyright © The McGraw-Hill Companies, Inc.

Name _____

Read the selection. Complete the Main Topic and Key Details chart.

Main Topic		
Detail	**Detail**	**Detail**

Copyright © The McGraw-Hill Companies, Inc.

Name _____

A. Read the draft model. Use the questions that follow the draft to help you add sequence words.

Draft Model

I saw a white tiger when I visited the zoo last summer. It was a very hot day, and the white tiger was panting. He splashed around in a lake that surrounded his pen. Caretakers threw him giant ice cubes. He licked and ate the cubes that contained fruit. He moved to a shady area of his pen.

---

1. What does the white tiger do first? What does he do next?

2. What event happens last?

3. What words can you add to make the writing easier to understand?

B. Now revise the draft by adding sequence words such as *first, next, then,* and *last* to help readers understand the order of events.

_____

_____

_____

_____

_____

Copyright © The McGraw-Hill Companies, Inc.

Name _____

In the Cave

The scientist enters the cave. It is cold and dim. She spies **shrimp** and **cave beetles**. These animals never leave the cave. Then she sees a **snail**. It may leave the cave at times.

Cave Animals	
Always live in caves: cave shrimp, cave beetle, and cave fish.	Sometimes live in caves: snail, spider, and worm.

Answer the questions about the text.

1. How can you tell that this text is narrative nonfiction?

_____

2. What happens after the scientist sees shrimp and cave beetles?

_____

3. Why are **shrimp**, **cave beetles**, and **snail** in bold print?

_____

4. What information can you get from the chart?

_____

Copyright © The McGraw-Hill Companies, Inc.

Name _____

> To figure out a new word, look for a **suffix**, or word part added to the end of the word.
>
> The suffix *-ful* means "full of."
>
> The suffix *-ly* means "in a way that is."

A. Underline the word that has a suffix in each sentence. Then write the word and its meaning.

1. Dr. Jones was hopeful that he would see animals.

   _____

2. He made a careful study of what he found.

   _____

3. He was greatly interested in comparing the two places.

   _____

B. Write a word that means the same as the group of words. Your new word will end in *-ful* or *-ly*.

4. full of play   5. in way that is clear

   _____   _____

Copyright © The McGraw-Hill Companies, Inc.

Name _____

Reread "Two Kinds of Tundra." Think about how the author used main topic and key details. Use the words and picture to help you complete the sentences below.

1. The main topic is _____

_____

_____.

2. The author describes Arctic and alpine tundras to explain

_____

_____.

3. In the section "The Arctic Tundra," the author includes the key

   detail _____

_____

_____

4. In the section "The Alpine Tundra," the author includes the key

   detail _____

_____

_____.

Copyright © The McGraw-Hill Companies, Inc.

Name _____

adult	alive	covered	fur
giant	groom	mammal	offspring

Choose the word that makes sense in each blank. Then write the word on the line.

1. A baby chick is _____ with soft feathers.

2. Some _____ look a lot like their parents.

3. Whales are _____ sea animals.

4. A cat will _____ itself to stay clean.

5. A horse is a _____ because it feeds its babies milk.

6. A fox's _____ coat helps to keep it warm.

7. Some baby animals need to be cared for by an _____.

8. Animals need food and water to stay _____.

Copyright © The McGraw-Hill Companies, Inc.

Name _____

A **consonant digraph** is two consonants together that stand for only one sound.

A. Say each picture name. Read the words and circle the word with the same beginning sound. Write the word.

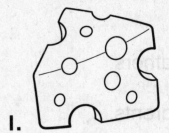

1.   chop   sting   _____

2.   pitch   while   _____

A **suffix** is a word part added to the end of a word to make a new word.
- The suffix *-ful* means "full of."
- The suffix *-less* means "without."

B. Read each word. Write its meaning.

3. helpless _____   4. careful _____

5. thankful _____   6. useless _____

Copyright © The McGraw-Hill Companies, Inc.

Name _____

Read the passage. Use the reread strategy to make sure you understand the information.

Opossums

     An adult opossum is about the size of a big cat. When
12 the mother gives birth, she may have seven or more
22 babies. She has a pouch like a kangaroo.

30   Each baby opossum is the size of a honeybee. At
40 first, they stay inside the mother's pouch. After about
49 two months, the babies leave the mother's pouch. They
58 are still small. The mother can carry the babies on her
69 back. The baby opossums grow quickly. Soon the young
78 animals are on their own.

Copyright © The McGraw-Hill Companies, Inc.

Name _____

Opossum

ear

nose

whiskers

tail

thumb

83   An adult opossum has long gray fur on its body.
93 Its face is white. It has black ears. The opossum has
104 a pointed snout with a pink nose. Its tail and feet are
116 pink, too. It has a mouth full of fifty sharp teeth.

127   An opossum has a very useful tail. This tail is almost
138 a foot long with very little hair. An opossum can use
149 this tail to grab onto things. Its tail helps it hold onto
161 tree branches. On each hind foot, an opossum has a
171 thumb. These thumbs help it grab onto things, too.

180   These animals are known for "playing possum."
187 When rattled by a predator, they lie still and don't move
198 at all until the threat goes away.

1996 PhotoDisc, Inc./Getty Images

Copyright © The McGraw-Hill Companies, Inc.

Name _____

A. Reread the passage and answer the questions.

I. What is the main topic of the passage?

_____

_____

2. What is a key detail about an adult opossum?

_____

_____

3. What is a key detail about a baby opossum?

_____

_____

B. Work with a partner. Read the passage aloud. Pay attention to pronunciation. Stop after one minute. Fill out the chart.

	Words Read	–	Number of Errors	=	Words Correct Score
First Read		–		=	
Second Read		–		=	

Copyright © The McGraw-Hill Companies, Inc.

Name _____

Read the selection. Complete the Main Topic and Key Details chart.

Main Topic		
Detail	**Detail**	**Detail**

Copyright © The McGraw-Hill Companies, Inc.

Name _____

A. Read the draft model. Use the questions that follow the draft to help you add linking words.

> ### Draft Model
>
> A puppy is the name for a baby dog. A puppy is much smaller than its parent. It is the same shape as its parent. It has fur like its parent. It cannot do many things for itself.

I. What are some ways you can connect the ideas in the draft?

2. How is a puppy different from its parent?

3. How is a puppy the same as its parent?

B. Now revise the draft by adding and replacing words to connect ideas with linking words, such as *and, so, also, but,* or *however*.

_____

_____

_____

_____

Copyright © The McGraw-Hill Companies, Inc.

Name _____

Leopards and Their Cubs

Leopard cubs are born with their eyes closed. Their fur is longer and thicker than their parents' fur. It is grayer, too. The cubs' spots are not easy to see.

Leopard

long tail

black spots

yellow eyes

whiskers

claws

Answer the questions about the text.

1. How do you know this is an expository text?

_____

_____

2. What information can you learn from looking at the diagram?

_____

3. What information can you learn by reading the labels?

_____

Copyright © The McGraw-Hill Companies, Inc.

Anup Shah/Photodisc/Getty Images

Name _____

> **Multiple-meaning words** have more than one meaning. Use other words in the sentence to figure out which meaning is being used.

Read each sentence. Figure out the meaning of the word in bold print. Put a checkmark in the box before the meaning that matches its use in the sentence.

1. The mother can carry the babies on her **back**.

☐ the part of the body opposite the front

☐ to move away from something

2. The opossum has a **pointed** snout with a pink nose.

☐ having a sharp end

☐ showed where something is

3. Soon the young animals are on their **own**.

☐ to have or hold as property

☐ for or by oneself

4. When **rattled** by a predator, they lie still and don't move at all until the threat goes away.

☐ made upset or disturbed

☐ made noise

Copyright © The McGraw-Hill Companies, Inc.

Name _____

Reread "Opossums." Write your opinion about how the author used details to support the main topic of the text. Use the words and picture to help you complete the sentences below.

I. The author wrote this text to tell about _____

_____

_____ .

2. I think the most important details are _____

_____ and

_____ .

3. The text feature is important because _____

_____

_____ .

Copyright © The McGraw-Hill Companies, Inc.

Name _____

behave	express
feathers	flapping

Use what you know about the words in the sentences to choose the word that makes sense in each blank. Then write the word on the line.

I. The crow has black _____.

_____

2. The bird is able to fly by _____ its wings.

_____

3. The children _____ by following the classroom rules.

_____

4. I _____ myself by writing in a journal.

_____

B. Choose one vocabulary word from the box above. Write the word in a sentence of your own.

5. _____

_____

Copyright © The McGraw-Hill Companies, Inc.

Name _____

> Three letters can be blended together such as ***scr, spl, spr, str, shr,*** and ***thr.*** Listen to the beginning sounds in ***scrap*** and ***split***.

A. Look at the picture. Write the missing blend for each word.

1. _____ one

2. _____ ash

3. _____ ub

4. _____ ing

5. _____ ap

6. _____ ub

> A **compound word** is made up of two smaller words.

B. Circle each compound word. Write the two smaller words that make it up.

7. beaches   bedspread   _____ _____

8. wishbone   wonder   _____ _____

9. springtime   spotted   _____ _____

Copyright © The McGraw-Hill Companies, Inc.

Name _____

Read the poem. Use the reread strategy to check your understanding.

A Tortoise

You will find that a tortoise is a mild fellow,

10   It lives a life that's calm and mellow.

18   A tortoise can live for quite a long span,

27   In fact it may even live longer than a man.

37   You'll never find a tortoise at sea,

44   It lives on land—that's where it should be.

53   Would a tortoise be able to win a race?

62   Not since it moves at such a slow pace.

71   It has four stumpy legs and four tortoise feet.

80   For a snack, plants are its favorite of treat.

Copyright © The McGraw-Hill Companies, Inc.

89   Some creatures have feathers and some have hair,

97   But what does our friend tortoise wear?

104   A tortoise wears a hard outer shell,

111   That always works to serve it well.

118   When a tortoise doesn't know where to hide,

126   It just pulls its head and four limbs inside.

135   Even though a tortoise may be shy,

142   It can walk around with its head held high.

151   For a tortoise is a marvel of the animal pack,

161   It carries its home right on its back.

Copyright © The McGraw-Hill Companies, Inc.

Name _____

A. Reread the passage and answer the questions.

I. How long can a tortoise live?

_____

_____

2. Where does a tortoise live?

_____

_____

3. How does a tortoise use its shell?

_____

_____

B. Work with a partner. Read the passage aloud. Pay attention to how you pause and group words together. Stop after one minute. Fill out the chart.

	Words Read	–	Number of Errors	=	Words Correct Score
First Read		–		=	
Second Read		–		=	

Copyright © The McGraw-Hill Companies, Inc.

Name _____

Read the selection. Complete the Key Details chart.

Detail	Detail	Detail

Copyright © The McGraw-Hill Companies, Inc.

Name _____

A. Read the draft model. Use the questions that follow the draft to help you think about what precise words you can add.

Draft Model

I went outside one night.
Something moved, so I turned on the light.
It was a little toad,
Hopping across the road.

I. What kind of night is it?

2. What does the toad look like?

3. How does the toad move?

B. Now revise the draft by adding precise words to give readers a clearer picture about the night and the toad.

_____

_____

_____

_____

Copyright © The McGraw-Hill Companies, Inc.

Name _____

The Robin

A robin gathers twigs and fluff,

And sticks and string and other stuff.

She chooses things she likes the best,

And weaves them in to build her nest.

Answer the questions about the text.

1. How do you know this text is a poem?

_____

_____

2. How many beats do you hear in each line?

_____

_____

3. Why do you think the poet uses rhythm?

_____

_____

Copyright © The McGraw-Hill Companies, Inc.

Name _____

> **Multiple-meaning words** have more than one meaning. Use other words in the sentence to figure out which meaning is being used.

Read the lines from the poem. Circle the meaning of the word in bold print.

I. You'll never find a tortoise at sea,
   It lives on **land**—that's where it should be.

   the ground   to come down from above

2. A tortoise wears a hard outer shell,
   That always works to serve it **well**.

   in a good way   a hole in the ground that stores water

3. It has four stumpy legs and four tortoise **feet**.

   measurements of 12 inches   parts of the body

4. When a tortoise doesn't know where to hide,
   It just pulls its head and four **limbs** inside.

   tree branches   legs

5. For a tortoise is a marvel of the animal **pack**,
   It carries its home right on its back.

   to put things in a suitcase   a group of animals

Copyright © The McGraw-Hill Companies, Inc.

Name _____

Reread "A Tortoise." Write an analysis of how the author used word choice to tell about tortoises. Use the words and picture to help you complete the sentences below.

I. The author wrote this poem to tell about _____

_____

_____

_____.

2. The words _____ and _____

rhyme. The poet uses rhyme to _____

_____

_____.

3. The poet helped me understand _____

_____

_____

by using the words _____

_____.

Copyright © The McGraw-Hill Companies, Inc.

Name _____

| amazing | force | measure | objects |
| proved | speed | true | weight |

A. Read each clue below. Then find the vocabulary word on the right that matches the clue. Draw a line from the clue to the word.

1. how heavy something is   **a.** speed

2. showed something is true   **b.** amazing

3. very surprising   **c.** weight

4. how fast something moves   **d.** force

5. not false   **e.** proved

6. things you can see and touch   **f.** measure

7. a push or a pull   **g.** objects

8. find the size of something   **h.** true

B. Choose one vocabulary word from the box above. Write the word in a sentence of your own.

9. _____

_____

Copyright © The McGraw-Hill Companies, Inc.

Name _____

> The letters *a, ai*, *ay*, *ea*, *ei*, *eigh*, and *ey* can stand for the long *a* sound. Listen to the vowel sound as you say the words **apron, pail**, **day**, **great**, **eight**, and **they**.

A. Read each row of words. Circle the long *a* word and write it on the line. Then underline the letters that spell the long *a* sound.

1. bike   jump   stay   _____

2. camp   nail   green   _____

3. weigh   mean   lock   _____

4. shell   prey   huge   _____

5. rein   rope   pick   _____

6. float   break   last   _____

7. snap   pump   baby   _____

> A **contraction** is a short way of writing two words. An apostrophe stands for the missing letters.

B. Write the contraction for each pair of words.

8. they have _____   9. she is _____

10. we are _____   11. you will _____

Copyright © The McGraw-Hill Companies, Inc.

Name _____

Read the passage. Use the reread strategy to check your understanding of new information or difficult facts.

Roller Coaster Science

	Riding a roller coaster can feel like flying. The cars
10	race up and down the track. They go around corners at
21	a high speed. Do you know how a roller coaster works?

32 The Ride Begins

35	A long chain runs under the first uphill track. A
45	motor moves this chain in a loop. It's like the moving
56	belt at the store checkout. The roller coaster cars grip
66	onto the chain. The chain pulls the roller coaster train
76	up to the top of the hill.

83 Moving Along the Track

87	The train reaches the top of the hill. The chain is
98	unhooked. **Gravity** takes the train down the track.
106	Gravity is a **force** that pulls objects toward the center of
117	the earth.

Copyright © The McGraw-Hill Companies, Inc.

Name _____

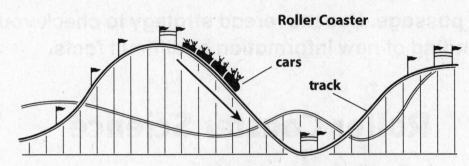

Roller Coaster

cars

track

Gravity moves the cars down the hill.

119   As the train moves down the track, it **speeds** up. It
130 goes faster and faster. This speed helps move the train
140 up the next hill. Then it all happens again.

149 **The Ride Ends**

152   When the ride is over, the roller coaster train must
162 stop. There are brakes built into the track. These brakes
172 stop the **motion** of the train. The roller coaster ends at
183 the same position it started.

188   That is the science of a roller coaster. Think about
198 these forces the next time you take a ride!

Copyright © The McGraw-Hill Companies, Inc.

Name _____

A. Reread the passage and answer the questions.

1. What is the topic of this passage?

_____

_____

2. What is one fact that the author includes about the topic?

_____

_____

3. What is the author's purpose for writing this passage?

_____

_____

B. Work with a partner. Read the passage aloud. Pay attention to how your voice rises and falls. Stop after one minute. Fill out the chart.

	Words Read	–	Number of Errors	=	Words Correct Score
First Read		–		=	
Second Read		–		=	

Copyright © The McGraw-Hill Companies, Inc.

Name _____

Read the selection. Complete the Author's Purpose chart.

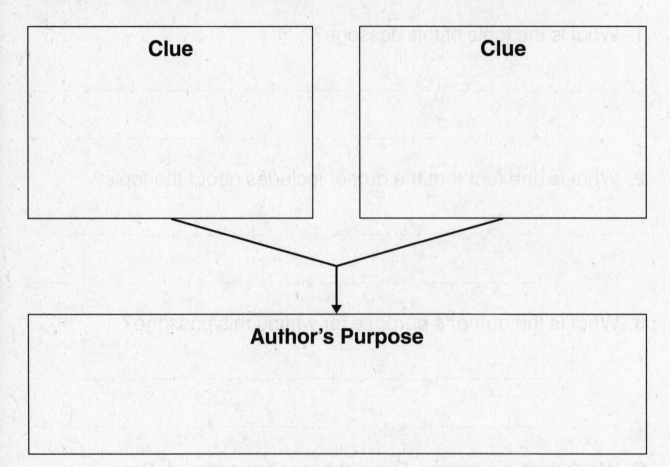

Clue	Clue

Author's Purpose

Copyright © The McGraw-Hill Companies, Inc.

Name _____

A. Read the draft model. Use the questions that follow the draft to add words that tell the order of the ideas.

Draft Model

You use the force of push and pull. When you throw the ball to a player, you use the force of push. When you try to take the ball from a player, you use the force of pull.

I. What words can you add to the first sentence to make it clearer?

2. What words can you add to the second sentence to make it clearer?

3. Does the order of ideas make sense?

B. Now revise the draft by adding words. Check that the order of ideas makes sense.

_____

_____

_____

_____

_____

Copyright © The McGraw-Hill Companies, Inc.

Name _____

How a Yo-Yo Works

Let a yo-yo go and it spins down as the string **unwinds**. It keeps spinning at the end of the string. With a quick tug, the string **rewinds** and the yo-yo climbs back up.

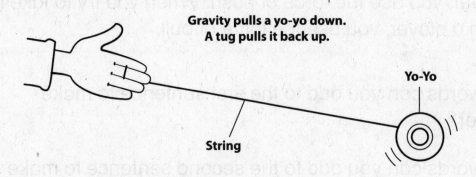

Gravity pulls a yo-yo down.
A tug pulls it back up.

Yo-Yo

String

Answer the questions about the text.

1. How do you know this is informational text?

_____

_____

2. Why are the words **unwinds** and **rewinds** in bold print?

_____

_____

3. What can you learn from the diagram?

_____

Copyright © The McGraw-Hill Companies, Inc.

Name _____

> A **simile** compares two unlike things. It uses the word *like* or *as* to make the comparison.

Read the sentences. Then answer the questions.

I. Riding a roller coaster can feel like flying.

What two things does the author compare?

_____

What does the simile mean?

_____

_____

2. A motor moves this chain in a loop. It is like the moving belt at the store checkout.

What two things does the author compare?

_____

What does the simile mean?

_____

3. The roller coaster's sound is as loud as thunder.

What two things does the author compare?

_____

What does the simile mean?

_____

Copyright © The McGraw-Hill Companies, Inc.

Name _____

Reread "Roller Coaster Science." Write about the author's purpose. Use the words and diagram to complete the sentences.

I. In _____,

the author wrote about _____

_____

_____

_____.

2. The author wrote this selection to _____

_____

_____.

3. The text feature the author used is a _____.

It helps the reader to _____

_____

_____.

Copyright © The McGraw-Hill Companies, Inc.

Name _____

| adventure | delighted | dreamed | enjoyed |
| grumbled | moonlight | neighbor | nighttime |

Read the story. Choose words from the box to complete the sentences. Then write the answers on the lines.

The sky got dark when _nighttime_ came. Max _grumbled_ that the end of the day was boring.

"Let's take a walk outside," said Mom. "The stars and _moonlight_ can light our way."

They walked down the street. Max was surprised and _delighted_ to see an owl fly by. They passed the house of a _neighbor_. There was a light shining in each window.

Max and Mom returned home. "What did you think of our night _adventure_?" asked Mom.

"I really _enjoyed_ it," said Max. I never _dreamed_ that night could be exciting!"

Copyright © The McGraw-Hill Companies, Inc.

Name _____

> The letters *i*, *y*, *igh*, and *ie* can stand for the long *i* sound. Listen to the vowel sound as you say the words *kind*, *why*, *might*, and *skies*.

A. Write the words in the box in the correct list below.

cry	light	wild	tie	high
sight	lie	dry	mind	try

I. words with the long *i* sound, as in *find*

_____ _____

2. words with the long *i* sound, as in *fly*

_____ _____ _____

3. words with the long *i* sound, as in *bright*

_____ _____ _____

4. words with the long *i* sound, as in *pie*

_____ _____

B. Draw a line to divide each word into syllables.

5. pony   **6.** table

7. spider   **8.** music

Copyright © The McGraw-Hill Companies, Inc.

Name _____

Read the passage. Use the reread strategy to check your understanding of story events.

A Shooting Star

Carla's family got to the park in the late afternoon.
10 The sun was shining in the blue sky. There was not a
22 cloud anywhere.

24 Carla and her sister Rosa were excited. It was their
34 first camping trip. They ran around the campsite. They
43 saw lots of big evergreen trees. A chipmunk ran on a
54 branch overhead.

56 Mama said, "Let's get things set up. Then we can go
67 for a hike."

70 Papa added, "We should have enough time to hike
79 before nightfall."

81 After the tents were set up, the family hiked. Daylight
91 was fading as they returned to the campsite.

99 "Look! There are fireflies here," said Carla.

Copyright © The McGraw-Hill Companies, Inc.

Name _____

106   Everyone looked up to watch the fireflies. Just then,
115 they saw a shooting star cross the dark night sky.

125   "What is that?" Rosa asked.

130   "It's a shooting star. Some people say you can wish
140 on a shooting star and your wish will come true,"
150 said Papa.

152   Carla and Rosa quickly made wishes.

158   Mama explained, "Some people call it a shooting star.
167 It's not a star, though. It's really just some dust flying
178 toward the earth. It heats up and glows. That's what
188 we see."

190   "No matter what we call it, I hope our wishes come
201 true!" said Carla.

Copyright © The McGraw-Hill Companies, Inc.

Name _____

A. Reread the passage and answer the questions.

1. What happens first in the story?

_____

_____

2. What happens after it gets dark?

_____

_____

3. What happens last?

_____

_____

B. Work with a partner. Read the passage aloud. Pay attention to how your voice rises and falls. Stop after one minute. Fill out the chart.

	Words Read	–	Number of Errors	=	Words Correct Score
First Read		–		=	
Second Read		–		=	

Copyright © The McGraw-Hill Companies, Inc.

Name _____

Read the selection. Complete the Sequence chart.

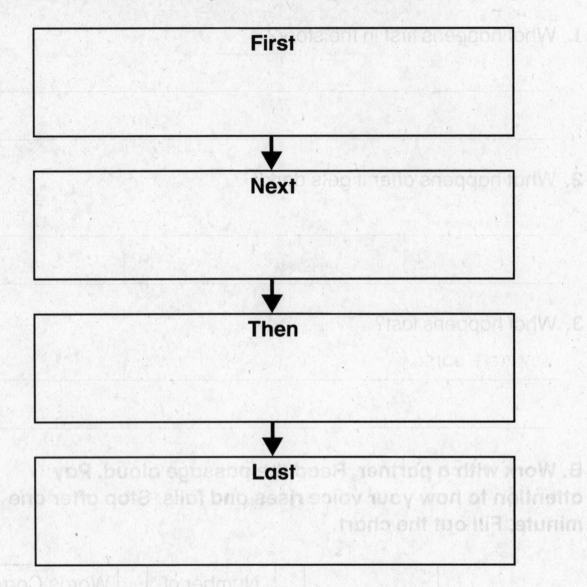

First

Next

Then

Last

Copyright © The McGraw-Hill Companies, Inc.

Name _____

A. Read the draft model. Use the questions that follow the draft to help you add words to connect ideas.

> ### Draft Model
>
> James and Dad were camping. The moonlight was bright. It shone on their tent. He saw the Big Dipper. The night was so dark. James dreamed he took a rocket ship so he could see more stars.

I. Which sentence already has a linking word in it?

2. What sentences can be combined to connect ideas?

3. What are some words you can use to show how the ideas are connected?

B. Now revise the draft by adding and replacing words to connect ideas with linking words, such as _and_, _so_, _but_, or _because_.

_____

_____

_____

_____

_____

Copyright © The McGraw-Hill Companies, Inc.

Name _____

Shapes in the Sky

One day, two friends named the cloud shapes they saw.

"Look at all the clouds in the sky. That one looks like a lion," said Grace.

"That cloud looks like a train," Marco said.

Answer the questions about the text.

1. How do you know this text is fiction?

_____

2. What is dialogue?

_____

3. What words does Grace say?

_____

4. What words does Marco say?

_____

Copyright © The McGraw-Hill Companies, Inc.

Name _____

> A **compound word** is a word made of two smaller words.

A. Read each sentence. Write the compound word. Draw a line between the two smaller words.

1. There was not a cloud anywhere. _____

2. They ran around the campsite. _____

3. They saw lots of big evergreen trees. _____

4. There are fireflies here. _____

B. Write the meaning of each compound word.

5. afternoon

_____

6. daylight

_____

7. everyone

_____

8. nightfall

_____

Copyright © The McGraw-Hill Companies, Inc.

Name _____

Reread "A Shooting Star." Write about how the author used sequence and illustrations to tell a story. Use the words and picture to complete the sentences.

1. At the beginning of the story, the author wrote that _____

_____

_____

_____

_____ .

2. In the middle, the author used an illustration to show _____

_____

_____

_____ .

3. At the end of the story, the author has Mama say that _____

_____ to show _____

_____

_____

_____ .

Copyright © The McGraw-Hill Companies, Inc.

Name _____

| across | borrow | countryside | idea |
| insists | lonely | solution | villages |

Choose the word that makes sense in each blank. Then write the word on the line.

1. The road passes through many small towns and _____.

2. We saw a sheep farm in the _____.

3. She felt _____ when everyone left the house.

4. May I please _____ your pencil?

5. The boy has a good _____ for his art project.

6. They use the bridge to get _____ the stream.

7. I know the _____ to this math problem.

8. The teacher _____ that students do their best.

Copyright © The McGraw-Hill Companies, Inc.

Name _____

The letters *o*, *oa*, *ow*, and *oe* can stand for the long *o* sound. Listen to the vowel sound as you say the words *so*, *road*, *low*, and *woe*.

A. Read each word in the box. Circle the words with the long *o* sound. Then underline the letter or letters that spell the long *o* sound.

drop	coat	told	mow	book
most	grow	loop	Joe	lost
toast	pond	show	toe	float

A **contraction** is a short way of writing two words. An apostrophe stands for the missing letters.

B. Write the two words that make up each contraction.

1. isn't _____   **2.** didn't _____

3. won't _____   **4.** aren't _____

Copyright © The McGraw-Hill Companies, Inc.

Name _____

Read the passage. Ask and answer questions as you read to check your understanding.

Helping Out in the Community

     Doug Long has been riding bikes for a long time.

10 When he was 16, he took a solo bike trip. He rode his

23 bike alone across the United States. That's a big journey

33 for a young man!

37   Now when Doug rides, it may be with a group of

48 children. Doug works with a volunteer group. The group

57 sets up bike rides for city kids. It gives the children time

69 to appreciate and enjoy the world around them. Doug

78 helps them explore nature.

82   Doug brings his own bike and helmet for a bike trip.

93 The children get bikes to ride and helmets to wear. Then

104 they go to a park or a nature area.

Copyright © The McGraw-Hill Companies, Inc.

Name _____

Doug Long helps children learn more about nature.

113   On one trip, the children saw a caterpillar. They
122 weren't sure if it was safe to touch it. Doug picked it up.
135 He showed it to the children. Once they were certain it
146 was harmless, they all took turns holding it.

154   Between bike trips, the children can learn how to fix
164 bikes. They can work at a bike workshop. This earns
174 them points. They can use the points to get a bike of
186 their own.

188   Doug Long likes to ride his bike. And he likes to help
200 out. He has made his community a better place.

Photo Courtesy of Doug Long and Trips for Kids

Copyright © The McGraw-Hill Companies, Inc.

Name _____

A. Reread the passage and answer the questions.

I. What did the author want you to know about Doug Long when Doug was 16?

_____

_____

2. What did the author want you to know about Doug's work with a volunteer group?

_____

_____

3. What is the author's purpose for writing this passage?

_____

_____

B. Work with a partner. Read the passage aloud. Pay attention to how you show feelings with your voice. Stop after one minute. Fill out the chart.

	Words Read	–	Number of Errors	=	Words Correct Score
First Read		–		=	
Second Read		–		=	

Copyright © The McGraw-Hill Companies, Inc.

Name _____

Read the selection. Complete the Author's Purpose chart.

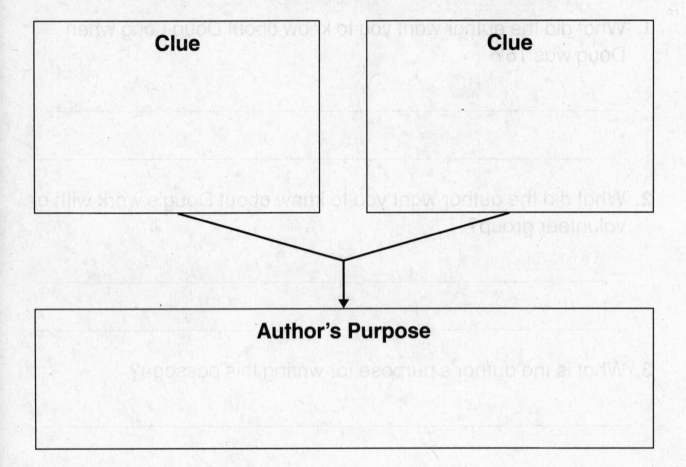

Copyright © The McGraw-Hill Companies, Inc.

Name _____

A. Read the draft model. Use the questions that follow the draft to help you add opinion words and phrases.

> ### Draft Model
>
> Last week my family went to the park. There was trash on the ground. We told friends and neighbors. We all helped clean it up. Now the park is nicer.

I. How do you think the writer feels about seeing trash at the park?

2. Why does everyone help clean up the trash?

3. How does everyone feel once the park is cleaned up?

B. Now revise the draft by adding opinion words and phrases to show how the writer feels about the topic.

_____

_____

_____

_____

_____

_____

_____

Copyright © The McGraw-Hill Companies, Inc.

Name _____

A Friendly City for Bikes

Sara Krause lives in Austin, Texas. The mayor asked her for ideas to improve bike safety. Now Sara and many other people have helped make Austin a friendly city for bikes.

Sara Krause was the leader of the bike safety group in Austin.

Answer the questions about the text.

I. How can you tell that this text is narrative nonfiction?

_____

_____

2. How has Sara Krause helped out in Austin?

_____

_____

3. Why does the author include a photo?

_____

4. What information can you learn from the caption?

_____

_____

John Krause

Copyright © The McGraw-Hill Companies, Inc.

Name _____

> **Synonyms** are words that have almost the same meaning.

A. Read each pair of sentences. Find the two words that are synonyms. Circle the synonyms and then write them on the lines.

1. When he was 16, he took a solo bike trip.
   He rode his bike alone across the United States.

   _____   _____

2. When he was 16, he took a solo bike trip.
   That's a big journey for a young man!

   _____   _____

3. Now when Doug rides, it may be with a group of children.
   The group sets up bike rides for city kids.

   _____   _____

B. Read the sentences. Write a word to answer each question.

They weren't sure if it was safe to touch it.
Once they were certain it was harmless, they all took turns holding it.

4. Which word in the second sentence is a synonym for **sure**?

   _____

5. Which word in the second sentence is a synonym for **safe**?

   _____

Copyright © The McGraw-Hill Companies, Inc.

Write About Reading: **Write an Analysis**

Name _____

Reread "Helping Out in the Community." Write about the author's purpose. Use the words and chart to complete the sentences.

I. In _____,

the author wrote about _____

_____

_____.

2. The author chose to write about Doug Long because _____

_____

_____

_____.

3. The author included the photo and caption to help the reader

_____

_____

_____

_____.

Copyright © The McGraw-Hill Companies, Inc.

Name _____

| damage | dangerous | destroy | event |
| harsh | prevent | warning | weather |

A. Use what you know about the definitions to choose the word that makes sense for each clue. Write the word on the line.

1. a sign of danger to come _____

2. something that happens _____

3. injury or harm that happens to something

   _____

4. what it is like outside at a certain time and place

   _____

5. to stop something from happening _____

6. not safe _____

7. rough or unpleasant _____

8. to break something so it can't be used _____

B. Choose one vocabulary word from the box above. Write the word in a sentence of your own.

9. _____

Copyright © The McGraw-Hill Companies, Inc.

Name _____

> The letters *e*, *ee*, *ea*, *ie*, *y*, *ey*, and *e_e* can stand for the long *e* sound. Listen to the vowel sound as you say the words *me*, *see*, *leap*, *field*, *happy*, *money*, and *eve*.

A. Read each row of words. Circle the long *e* word and write it on the line. Then underline the letters that spell the long *e* sound.

1. must   leaf   sleigh   _____

2. chief   track   vase   _____

3. bee   rest   home   _____

4. they   drum   pony   _____

5. steak   we   block   _____

6. keys   spend   wise   _____

> Add *-s* to form the plural of most nouns.
>
> If a word ends in a consonant plus *y*, change the *y* to *i* and add *-es* to form the plural.

B. Write each word to make it plural.

7. puppy _____   8. clock _____

9. baby _____   10. nest _____

Copyright © The McGraw-Hill Companies, Inc.

Name _____

Read the passage. Ask and answer questions as you read to check your understanding.

Ice Hotels

How would you like to stay in an ice hotel? There
11 really are such places in cold climates.

18 **What Is an Ice Hotel?**

23 An ice hotel is like a big **igloo**. The walls are made of
36 snow and ice. The furniture and art are made of ice, too.

48 **How Is an Ice Hotel Built?**

54 In some cold places, people build ice hotels. They
63 wait until winter because summer is too warm. Builders
72 choose a spot near a frozen river. Workers cut many ice
83 blocks to build walls. They use **snice** to keep the blocks
94 from coming apart. This is a mix of snow and ice that
106 holds everything together.

109 When they are done with the outside walls, workers
118 move to the inside. They carve furniture from blocks
127 of ice. They carve works of art, too. All this work takes
139 time. A large ice hotel can take five to six weeks to build.

Copyright © The McGraw-Hill Companies, Inc.

Name _____

152 **Staying in an Ice Hotel**

157   People must bundle up to stay in an ice hotel. The
168 **temperature** inside must stay below freezing. If it gets
177 above freezing, the ice could melt.

183   People sleep in thick sleeping bags on ice beds. They
193 sit on ice chairs. They even drink from ice glasses.

203 **What Happens to an Ice Hotel?**

209   An ice hotel only stands while it is cold. Once spring
220 comes, the hotel melts. The water returns to the river.
230 Then builders must wait until winter when the water
239 freezes to build the next ice hotel.

Copyright © The McGraw-Hill Companies, Inc.

Name _____

A. Reread the passage and answer the questions.

1. What is one key detail from the passage?

_____

_____

2. What is another key detail from the passage?

_____

_____

3. What is the main idea of the passage?

_____

_____

B. Work with a partner. Read the passage aloud. Pay attention to where you pause. Stop after one minute. Fill out the chart.

	Words Read	–	Number of Errors	=	Words Correct Score
First Read		–		=	
Second Read		–		=	

Copyright © The McGraw-Hill Companies, Inc.

Name _____

Read the selection. Complete the Main Idea and Key Details chart.

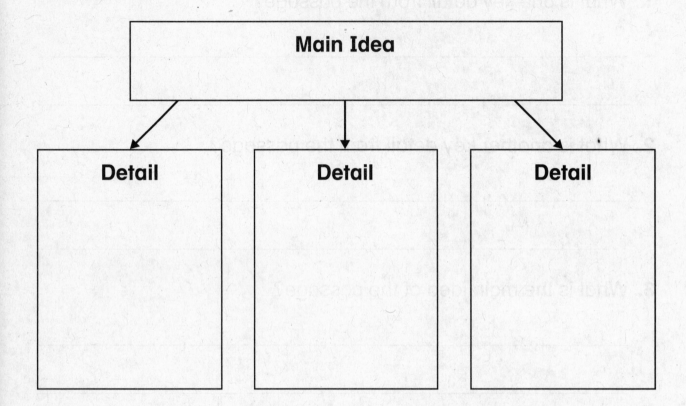

Copyright © The McGraw-Hill Companies, Inc.

Name _____

A. Read the draft model. Use the questions that follow the draft to help you add a strong conclusion.

> **Draft Model**
>
> A weather forecaster tells people about the weather in the area. She tells how hot or cold it is. She can also warn about bad weather.

I. What is the topic of the writing?

2. What is the main idea?

3. What information could you include in a conclusion sentence?

B. Now revise the draft by adding a strong conclusion to sum up the writing and tell the main idea.

_____
_____
_____
_____
_____
_____

Copyright © The McGraw-Hill Companies, Inc.

Name _____

Drought

A **drought** is a long period of dry weather. Little or no rain falls during a drought. Without water, farmers' crops stop growing. The **water supply** for people gets low, too.

What to Do in a Drought
1. Use only the water you need.
2. Make sure there are no leaky faucets.
3. Take shorter showers.
4. Water outdoor plants and lawns when it is cold.

Answer the questions about the text.

1. How do you know that this is expository text?

_____

_____

2. Why are the words **drought** and **water supply** in bold print?

_____

_____

3. What can you learn from the sidebar?

_____

Copyright © The McGraw-Hill Companies, Inc.

Name _____

> **Antonyms** are words that have opposite meanings.

A. Read each pair of sentences. Find the two words that are antonyms. Circle the antonyms and then write them on the lines.

1. They use snice to keep the blocks from coming apart.
   This is a mix of snow and ice that holds everything together.

   _____   _____

2. The workers finish the outside walls.
   Then they move to the inside.

   _____   _____

3. The shelf above the bed is made of ice.
   There is more ice below the bed.

   _____   _____

4. Once spring comes, the hotel melts.
   Then builders must wait until winter when the water freezes to build the next ice hotel.

   _____   _____

Copyright © The McGraw-Hill Companies, Inc.

Name _____

Reread "Ice Hotels." Write your opinion about how the author used details to support the main idea of the text. Use the words and picture to help you complete the sentences below.

1. The author wrote this text to _____

_____

_____

_____.

2. I think the most important details are _____

_____ and _____

_____

_____

_____.

3. These details are important because _____

_____

_____

_____

_____.

Copyright © The McGraw-Hill Companies, Inc.

Name _____

cheered	concert	instruments	movements
music	rhythm	sounds	understand

Use what you know about the words in the sentences to choose the word that makes sense in each blank. Then write the word on the line.

1. A swimmer kicks with strong leg _____.

2. My sister listens to country _____.

3. The band played my favorite song at the _____.

4. I use a dictionary if I don't _____ a word.

5. Pianos are _____ that have keys.

6. He taps the _____ of the song on his drum.

7. The rusty wheel made squeaking _____ as it turned.

8. The crowd _____ for their favorite team.

Copyright © The McGraw-Hill Companies, Inc.

Name _____

> The letters *u_e*, *ew*, *ue*, and *u* can stand for the long *u* sound. Listen to the vowel sound as you say the words **use**, **mew**, **hue**, and **menu**.

A. Read each word in the box. Circle the words with the long *u* sound. Then underline the letter or letters that spell the long *u* sound.

fuel	mule	just	few	bunch
cues	unit	jump	trunk	fumes
lucky	music	cube	pew	huge

> The ending *-er* is added to an adjective to compare two nouns. The ending *-est* is added to an adjective to compare more than two nouns.

B. Write each word and ending to make a new word. Write it on the lines.

1. strong + est

_____

2. few + er

_____

3. kind + er

_____

4. slow + est

_____

Copyright © The McGraw-Hill Companies, Inc.

Name _____

Read the passage. Ask and answer questions as you read to check your understanding.

Making Music

There are different ways to make music. Let's learn
09 about some musical instruments. You might find some
17 of these in your school music group.

24 **Piano**

25   A piano is a musical instrument that has 88 keys. To
36 play the piano, you press keys on the keyboard. This
46 action moves wooden hammers. The hammers then hit
54 steel strings. The strings vibrate and make sound. When
63 the strings stop moving, the sound is discontinued.

71 **Violin**

72   A violin is in the string family of instruments. It is a
84 hollow wooden box. It has four strings running from top
94 to bottom. To play the violin, you pull the bow across
105 the strings. Or you can pluck the strings with a finger.
116 When the strings vibrate, they make sound.

Copyright © The McGraw-Hill Companies, Inc.

Name _____

Instruments in School Music Group

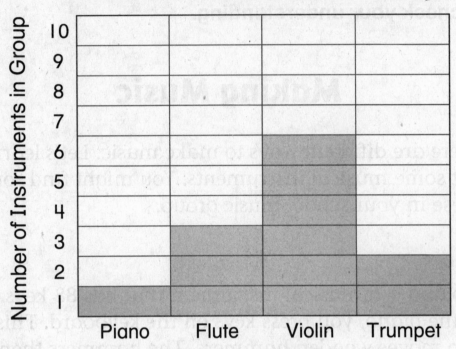

123 **Flute**

124   A flute is a woodwind instrument. It is a narrow tube
135 with finger holes. To make a sound on the flute, you
146 blow across an oval hole near the end. Sound bounces
156 off the edge of the hole and through the tube. To change
168 notes, cover and uncover the finger holes.

175 **Trumpet**

176   A trumpet is a brass instrument. It is a long, metal
187 tube with a loop. One end is shaped like a bell. It
199 has an uneven number of valves, three. To play the
209 trumpet, you buzz your lips into the mouthpiece. Move
218 the valves to change the notes.

224   Now let's review the instruments we read about.
232 Which would you like to play? No one can disagree.
242 There is a whole world of music to be made!

Copyright © The McGraw-Hill Companies, Inc.

Name _____

A. Reread the passage and answer the questions.

1. What is one key detail that is included in the passage?

_____

_____

2. What is another key detail that is included in the passage?

_____

_____

3. What is the main idea of the passage?

_____

_____

B. Work with a partner. Read the passage aloud. Pay attention to pronunciation. Stop after one minute. Fill out the chart.

	Words Read	−	Number of Errors	=	Words Correct Score
First Read		−		=	
Second Read		−		=	

Copyright © The McGraw-Hill Companies, Inc.

Name _____

Read the selection. Complete the Main Idea and Key Details chart.

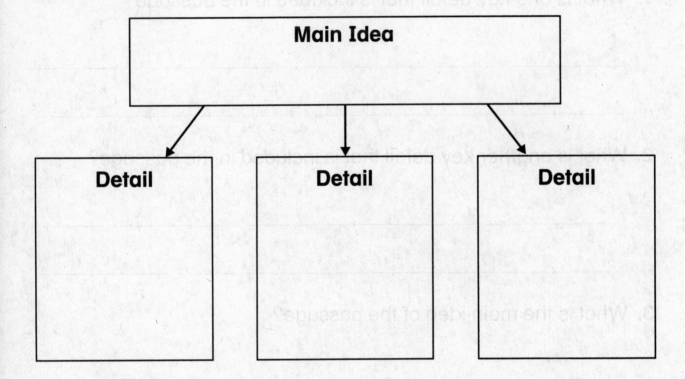

Main Idea

Detail

Detail

Detail

Copyright © The McGraw-Hill Companies, Inc.

Name _____

A. Read the draft model. Use the questions that follow the draft to help you think about using sentences of different lengths.

> **Draft Model**
>
> The musician gets her fiddle. She gets ready to play. She tunes up the fiddle. She sets up her sheet music. She plays a lively song.

1. Which sentences could you make longer?

2. Which sentences could you combine?

3. How can you make the sentences flow from one to the next?

B. Now revise the draft by writing sentences of different lengths.

_____

_____

_____

_____

_____

Copyright © The McGraw-Hill Companies, Inc.

Name _____

Warm Up to Sing

Many singers warm up their voice before they sing. This stretches out their muscles. Humming is one way to warm up. Blowing air through the lips is another way. Singing the musical scales warms up the voice, too.

Minutes

15			
10		▓	▓
5	▓	▓	▓
Warm-Up Exercise	Humming	Lips	Scales

Answer the questions about the text.

1. How do you know this is expository text?

_____

_____

2. What information can you learn from the bar graph?

_____

_____

3. How much time do singers spend singing scales?

_____

_____

Copyright © The McGraw-Hill Companies, Inc.

Name _____

> To figure out a new word, look for a **prefix**, or word part, at the beginning of the word.
>
> The prefix *re-* means "again."
>
> The prefix *un-* means "not."
>
> The prefix *dis-* means "opposite of."

Read each sentence. Underline the word that has a prefix. Then write the word and its meaning.

1. When the strings stop moving, the sound is discontinued.

   _____

2. You cover and uncover the finger holes using the keys.

   _____

3. It has an uneven number of valves, three.

   _____

4. Now let's review the instruments we read about.

   _____

5. No one can disagree.

   _____

Copyright © The McGraw-Hill Companies, Inc.

Name _____

Reread "Making Music." Write about how the author used details to support the main idea of the text. Use the words and picture to help you complete the sentences below.

1. The author wrote this text to _____

_____

_____

_____

_____ .

2. I think the most important details are _____

_____ and _____

_____

_____

_____ .

3. These details are important because _____

_____

_____

_____

_____ .

Copyright © The McGraw-Hill Companies, Inc.

Name _____

eerie	growth	layers	lively
location	region	seasons	temperate

Choose the word from the box that makes sense in each blank. Then write the word on the line.

I. This high area of the country is the mountain

_____.

2. A _____ of wildflowers fills the meadow.

3. Our class had a _____ party at the end of the year.

4. The weather is different in the winter and summer

_____.

5. The empty house gave us an _____ feeling.

6. The gardener digs down through _____ of sand and dirt.

7. It is not too hot or cold in a _____ climate.

8. Where is the _____ of your town on the map?

Copyright © The McGraw-Hill Companies, Inc.

Name _____

In some letter pairs, one of the letters is silent.

In **wr**, the **w** is silent as   In **kn**, the **k** is silent as
in **wrong**.   in **know**.

In **gn**, the **g** is silent as in **gnat**.

A. Choose two words from the box that have the same silent letter as each of the words below. Write the words on the line.

wrap	gnu	knife	wrist	knock	gnome

I. write   _____ _____

2. knot   _____ _____

3. gnaw   _____ _____

• The prefix **re-** means "again."

• The prefixes **un-** and **dis-** mean "not" or "opposite of."

• The suffix **-ful** means "full of", **-less** means "without."

B. Read each word. Write its meaning.

4. playful _____   7. dishonest _____

5. unsafe _____   8. sleepless _____

6. resend _____

Copyright © The McGraw-Hill Companies, Inc.

Name _____

Read the passage. Use the reread strategy to check your understanding of new information or difficult facts.

In a Redwood Forest

     A forest is a large area of land covered by trees
11 growing close together. There are different kinds of
19 forests. Some have hardwoods. These forests have trees
27 that lose their leaves each year. Some forests have
36 evergreen trees with needles. One of the most amazing
45 kinds of forests is the redwood forest.

52 **What Is a Redwood Tree?**

57   In a redwood forest, you will find some of the tallest
68 trees in the world. A redwood tree can grow over
78 300 feet tall. That's as tall as a 35-story skyscraper, a
90 building found in big cities.

95   Redwoods are some of the oldest trees in the world.
105 A redwood tree can live to be 2,000 years old. One
116 reason is these trees can survive fire. Their thick bark
126 keeps them from burning.

Copyright © The McGraw-Hill Companies, Inc.

Name _____

130 **Where Are Redwoods Found?**

134   Redwood forests are not found everywhere. California
141 is the only place where they grow in nature. Redwoods
151 need a wet climate to grow. The coast of California is a
163 good spot.

165   There is fog almost every day. The fog keeps the soil
176 moist. It also helps the redwood trees get water. They
186 soak up water from the fog right into their leaves.

196   In the past, people cut down many redwood trees.
205 These big trees would have disappeared. Now most of
214 them are protected in parks. They can't be destroyed
223 anymore. People can visit the parks to see these special
233 forests.

Copyright © The McGraw-Hill Companies, Inc.

Name _____

A. Reread the passage and answer the questions.

I. How are some forests different from others?

_____

_____

2. How is a redwood tree like a 35-story skyscraper?

_____

_____

3. How was the past different for redwood trees than today?

_____

_____

B. Work with a partner. Read the passage aloud. Pay attention to pronunciation. Stop after one minute. Fill out the chart.

	Words Read	−	Number of Errors	=	Words Correct Score
First Read		−		=	
Second Read		−		=	

Copyright © The McGraw-Hill Companies, Inc.

Name _____

Read the selection. Complete the Compare and Contrast chart.

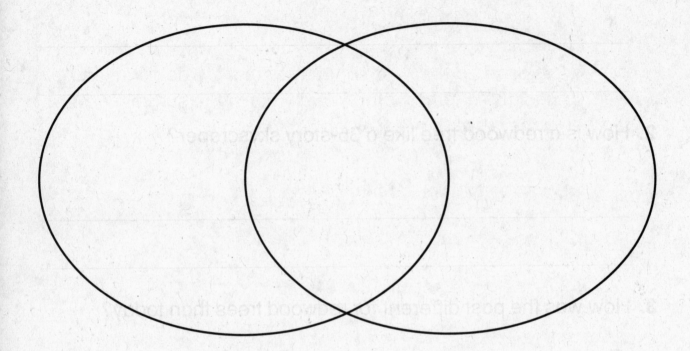

Copyright © The McGraw-Hill Companies, Inc.

Name _____

A. Read the draft model. Use the questions that follow the draft to help you think about the topic and ideas connected to it.

> **Draft Model**
>
> Some animals here in New Mexico are different from those in Alaska. We don't have moose or caribou, but we do have black bears and elk. The temperature is very hot in the summer. The weather in the winter can be much cooler.

I. What is the topic of the writing?

2. Which ideas connect to the topic?

3. Which ideas do not tell about the topic?

B. Now revise the draft by deleting sentences that do not connect to the topic. Add a new sentence that does connect to the topic.

_____

_____

_____

_____

_____

Copyright © The McGraw-Hill Companies, Inc.

Name _____

The Oasis of Mara

The Oasis of Mara is a place with water in the dry Mojave Desert. The water comes from underground. Plants can grow there. Native Americans once lived there.

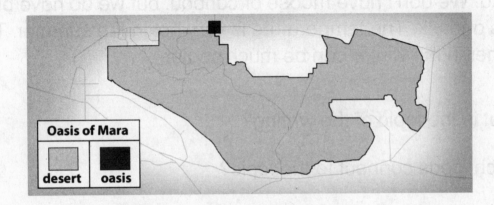

Answer the questions about the text.

I. How do you know this is expository text?

_____

_____

2. What is the Oasis of Mara?

_____

_____

3. What does the map show you?

_____

_____

Copyright © The McGraw-Hill Companies, Inc.

Name _____

> A **compound word** is a word made of two smaller words.

Read each sentence. Write the compound word and draw a line between the two smaller words. Then write the meaning of the compound word.

1. Some have hardwoods. _____

_____

2. Some forests have evergreen trees with needles. _____

_____

3. One of the most amazing kinds of forest is the redwood

forest. _____

_____

4. That's as tall as a 35-story skyscraper. _____

_____

5. These forests are not found everywhere. _____

_____

Copyright © The McGraw-Hill Companies, Inc.

Name _____

Reread "In a Redwood Forest." Write about how the author used text features.

I. This story is expository because the author wrote about _____

_____

_____

_____.

2. I know it is expository because the author included text features,

such as _____

_____

_____

_____.

3. These text features help readers because _____

_____

_____

_____.

Copyright © The McGraw-Hill Companies, Inc.

Name _____

| active | earth | explode | island |
| local | properties | solid | steep |

A. Read each clue below. Then find the vocabulary word on the right that matches the clue. Draw a line from the clue to the word.

1. something that is nearby   **a.** properties

2. land with water all around it   **b.** active

3. burst loudly with a lot of force   **c.** steep

4. having a very sharp slope   **d.** island

5. something that is moving   **e.** local

6. the traits of something   **f.** earth

7. the ground or land we walk on   **g.** solid

8. hard and firm   **h.** explode

B. Choose one vocabulary word from the box above. Write the word in a sentence of your own.

9. _____

_____

Copyright © The McGraw-Hill Companies, Inc.

Name _____

> The letters **er**, **ir**, **ur**, and **or** can stand for the same sound.
> You can hear the sound as you say the words **fern**, **third**, **burn**,
> and **world**.

**A. Circle the word that has the vowel sound spelled *er, ir,
ur*, or *or*. Write the two letters that make the vowel sound
on the line.**

I. cuts   curve   race   _____

2. her   rub   ring   _____

3. rise   worse   wrap   _____

4. string   wrist   first   _____

> Before adding **-s**, **-es**, **-ed**, or **-ing** to some verbs with short
> vowels, double the final consonant.
>
> Before adding **-s**, **-es**, **-ed**, or **-ing** to some verbs with long
> vowels ending in *e*, drop the final *e*.
>
> Before adding **-s**, **-es**, **-ed**, or **-ing** to some verbs ending in
> *y*, change *y* to *i*.

B. Write each word with the ending shown.

5. race + ed = _____   6. keep + s = _____

7. hurry + es = _____   8. trip + ing = _____

Copyright © The McGraw-Hill Companies, Inc.

Name _____

Read the passage. Use the reread strategy to check your understanding of new information or difficult facts.

Tsunamis

What Is a Tsunami?

4   You may have seen big **waves** at the beach. Now
14   imagine waves that reach a height of over 100 feet tall!
25   Tsunamis are a set of ocean waves that rush over land.
36   The waves look like giant walls of water.

44   Tsunamis have different **causes**. One event is an
52   undersea earthquake that causes the ocean floor to
60   move and shake. Other causes are underwater landslides
68   or volcanoes. These strong actions build tsunami waves.
76   The waves head for shore, the land along the ocean.

86   When the tsunami waves start, they may be just one
96   foot high. They extend, or reach, deep down into the
106 ocean.

Copyright © The McGraw-Hill Companies, Inc.

Name _____

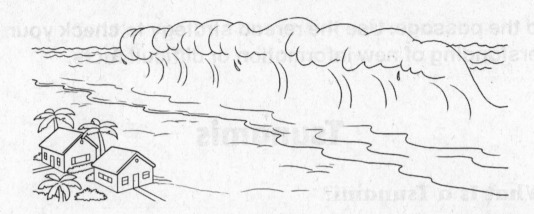

107   The waves travel toward shore. The waves can move
116 up to 500 miles per hour. That's as fast as a jet plane.

129   As the waves reach shallow water near land, they slow
139 down. They start to squeeze together. This pushes them
148 higher. Then the big waves hit the shore.

156 Damage from a Tsunami

160   Tsunamis cause lots of damage and harm. They can
169 hurt people. They can smash houses and knock down
178 trees. They can cause flooding. They can make drinking
187 water unsafe.

189 Tsunami Warnings

191   There are systems in place to warn, or tell, people
201 about tsunamis. People find out the big waves are
210 coming. Then they move to higher ground to stay safe
220 from the tsunamis.

Copyright © The McGraw-Hill Companies, Inc.

Name _____

A. Reread the passage and answer the questions.

I. What three things can cause a tsunami?

_____

_____

2. What is the effect when the waves get to shallow water near the land?

_____

_____

3. What happens when people get a tsunami warning?

_____

_____

B. Work with a partner. Read the passage aloud. Pay attention to where you pause and how you group words together. Stop after one minute. Fill out the chart.

	Words Read	–	Number of Errors	=	Words Correct Score
First Read		–		=	
Second Read		–		=	

Copyright © The McGraw-Hill Companies, Inc.

Name _____

Read the selection. Complete the Cause and Effect chart.

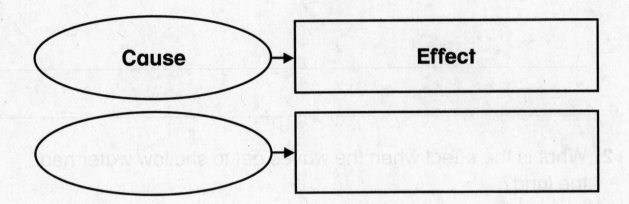

Copyright © The McGraw-Hill Companies, Inc.

Name _____

A. Read the draft model. Use the questions that follow the draft to help you add time-order words.

> ### Draft Model
>
> Some beaches have steep cliffs of rock. Waves crash into the rock. Tiny pieces of rock wash away. The top of the cliff can fall into the sea.

I. What happens first in the process of beach erosion, or washing away? What happens next?

2. What event happens last?

3. What time-order words can you add to make the order of events more clear?

B. Now revise the draft by adding time-order words such as *first, next, after,* and *last* to help readers understand the order of events.

_____

_____

_____

_____

_____

_____

Copyright © The McGraw-Hill Companies, Inc.

Name _____

Avalanche

An **avalanche** is a snow slide. High on a mountain, a big **chunk** of snow breaks loose. This snow slides down the **slope**, moving fast. It piles up at the bottom of the mountain.

Answer the questions about the text.

1. How do you know this is expository text?

   _____

   _____

2. Why are the words **avalanche**, **chunk**, and **slope** in bold print?

   _____

3. What is the cause of an avalanche?

   _____

4. What is the effect of an avalanche?

   _____

   _____

Copyright © The McGraw-Hill Companies, Inc.

Name _____

> Look at this example of **context clues** in a sentence. The underlined words explain what *height* means.
>
> Now imagine waves that reach a **height** of over 100 feet tall!

Read each sentence. Write the meaning of the word in bold print. Underline the context clues in the sentence that helped you.

1. **Tsunamis** are a set of ocean waves that rush over land.

    _____

2. One event is an undersea **earthquake** that causes the ocean floor to move and shake.

    _____

3. They **extend**, or reach, deep down into the ocean.

    _____

4. The waves head for **shore**, the land along the ocean.

    _____

5. Tsunamis cause lots of **damage** and harm.

    _____

Copyright © The McGraw-Hill Companies, Inc.

Name _____

Reread "Tsunamis." Write about how the author uses cause and effect.

1. In "Tsunamis," the author uses cause and effect to explain

   _____

   _____

   _____ .

2. One cause of a tsunami is _____

   _____

   _____ .

3. Some effects of tsunamis are _____

   _____

   _____ .

4. The author's use of cause and effect helped me understand

   _____

   _____

   _____ .

Copyright © The McGraw-Hill Companies, Inc.

Name _____

common	costume	customs	favorite
parades	surrounded	travels	wonder

Read the story. Choose words from the box to complete the sentences. Then write the answers on the lines.

My family _____ around the

country. We see different _____ and

celebrations wherever we go.

We visited a town that is _____

by farms. In summer the people gather in a shared space,

or _____ area for a harvest fair.

We also visited a city that has many

_____ in the streets. The marching

clowns are my _____ part. Each

clown wears a funny _____.

I _____ what we will see next!

Copyright © The McGraw-Hill Companies, Inc.

Name _____

> The letters **or**, **ore**, and **oar** can make the same sound. You can hear the sound in the words **short**, **chore**, and **soar**.
>
> The letters **ar** can stand for the sound you hear in the word **arm**.

A. Read the words in the box. Circle the letters that stand for the vowel sound. Then write each word below the picture with the same vowel sound.

> park   roar   scarf   yard   score   north

1. _____   4. _____

2. _____   5. _____

3. _____   6. _____

> Some nouns change their spelling to name more than one, as in **man** and **men**.

B. Write the plural form for each word.

7. tooth _____   8. child _____

Copyright © The McGraw-Hill Companies, Inc.

Name _____

Read the passage. Use the visualize strategy to form pictures in your mind about what happens in the story.

Giving Thanks Two Times

It was a cool November day. The dim sun hung like
11 a nickel in the sky. My friend Riku and I were walking
23 home from school. I hugged my arms when I felt
33 a breeze as sharp as a knife.

40 That day at school, we had studied Thanksgiving.
48 We learned that the early settlers celebrated their first
57 harvest at this very time of year. They had a big feast to
70 give thanks for all they had.

76 "My dad bought a turkey as big as a pillow. Are you
88 having a big turkey for Thanksgiving?" I asked Riku.

97 He grinned wide as he answered. "Yes, we're having a
107 turkey. And we're having rice, too!"

Copyright © The McGraw-Hill Companies, Inc.

Name _____

113   Riku explained that his family was celebrating Labor
121   Day Thanksgiving. It was a holiday in Japan, where
130   his family had lived. He told me that this holiday was a
142   harvest celebration, just like American Thanksgiving.

148   "Both holidays are in November, too!" I exclaimed.

156   Riku told me that last year he missed American
165   Thanksgiving. He had spent Labor Day Thanksgiving
172   in Japan. He was visiting his grandparents. He saw
181   parades. There were displays of fruits and vegetables,
189   like colorful rainbows.

192   "That was to give thanks for good crops," explained
201   Riku.

202   "You're lucky," I said. "You get to have two
211   Thanksgivings."

212   Riku said, "Why don't you visit my family for
221   Labor Day Thanksgiving? Then you can have two
229   Thanksgivings also!"

Copyright © The McGraw-Hill Companies, Inc.

Name _____

A. Reread the passage and answer the questions.

1. How are Thanksgiving and Labor Day Thanksgiving alike?

_____

_____

2. How are Thanksgiving and Labor Day Thanksgiving different?

_____

_____

3. How do the narrator and Riku celebrate their holidays in the same way?

_____

_____

B. Work with a partner. Read the passage aloud. Pay attention to how you use your voice to show feelings. Stop after one minute. Fill out the chart.

	Words Read	–	Number of Errors	=	Words Correct Score
First Read		–		=	
Second Read		–		=	

Copyright © The McGraw-Hill Companies, Inc.

Name _____

Read the selection. Complete the Compare and Contrast chart.

Copyright © The McGraw-Hill Companies, Inc.

Name _____

A. Read the draft model. Use the questions that follow the draft to help you add words, descriptions, and punctuation to show the writer's feelings.

Draft Model

Dear Frank,

    Last week I went to a Cinco de Mayo celebration. There was music and dancing. Bands played Mexican music. People wore costumes. There was even Mexican food.

                    Your friend,

                    Maxine

---

1. How does the writer feel about the celebration?

2. What words might describe the music, dancing, and costumes?

3. Where can you add punctuation to show how the writer feels?

B. Now revise the draft by adding words, descriptions, and punctuation to show how the writer feels about the Cinco de Mayo celebration.

_____

_____

_____

_____

Copyright © The McGraw-Hill Companies, Inc.

Name _____

Going to School

My name is Alba. I go to school in Mexico. I study six subjects, including Spanish and English. At lunchtime, I buy food at the school store and eat outside with my friends.

Answer the questions about the text.

1. How can you tell that this is realistic fiction?

_____

_____

2. Who is telling the story? How do you know?

_____

_____

_____

3. What is one realistic event that Alba tells about?

_____

_____

_____

Copyright © The McGraw-Hill Companies, Inc.

Name _____

> A **simile** compares two unlike things. It uses the word *like* or *as* to make the comparison.

Read the sentences. Then answer the questions.

I. The dim sun hung like a nickel in the sky.

What two things does the author compare? _____

_____

What does the simile mean? _____

_____

2. My dad bought a turkey as big as a pillow.

What two things does the author compare? _____

_____

What does the simile mean? _____

_____

3. There were displays of fruits and vegetables, like colorful rainbows.

What two things does the author compare? _____

_____

What does the simile mean? _____

_____

Copyright © The McGraw-Hill Companies, Inc.

Name _____

Reread "Giving Thanks Two Times." Complete the sentences by writing about how the author used comparing and contrasting. Use text evidence.

1. In "Giving Thanks Two Times," the author compares and contrasts

_____

_____

_____.

2. They are different because _____

_____

_____

_____.

3. They are alike because _____

_____

_____

_____.

4. The author's use of compare and contrast in this story helped

me understand _____

_____

_____.

Copyright © The McGraw-Hill Companies, Inc.

Name _____

ashamed	boast	dash	holler
plenty	similarities	victory	wisdom

Write the word on the line that makes sense.

1. There are _____ of books to read at the library.

2. The girl had to _____ to class when the bell rang.

3. The team is proud of their _____ in the game.

4. Can you name the _____ between a frog and a toad?

5. The man used his _____ to make the right choice.

6. The student felt _____ about not telling the truth.

7. The fans _____ loudly at the game.

8. She likes to _____ about her smart puppy.

Copyright © The McGraw-Hill Companies, Inc.

Name _____

> The letters **eer**, **ere**, and **ear** can stand for the **same** sound. Listen to the sound as you say the words **steer**, **here**, and **clear**.

A. Read each word. Circle the words that rhyme with the first word.

I. **year**   fern   mere   spear   jeer

2. **peer**   perk   cheer   near   fear

3. **here**   dear   herd   veer   ear

> An abbreviation is a short way to write a word. It begins with a capital letter and ends with a period.

B. Read each sentence. Write the underlined name on the line, using the correct abbreviation.

I. <u>Mister Flint</u> is a teacher.   _____

2. The school is on <u>North Street</u>.   _____

3. My friend lives on <u>Turner Avenue</u>.   _____

4. <u>Doctor Lopez</u> cares for pets.   _____

Copyright © The McGraw-Hill Companies, Inc.

Name _____

Read the passage. Use the visualize strategy to form pictures in your mind about what happens in the play.

Coyote Brings Fire

Characters

Narrator	Coyote	Squirrel
Chipmunk	Frog	Two Fire Beings

Narrator: Long ago, people did not have fire. Coyote
9 decided to bring it to them.

15 (Coyote speaks to Squirrel, Chipmunk, and Frog.)

22 **Coyote:** I know where we can get fire. The Fire Beings
33 have it at their camp. I have a workable plan to take the
46 fire. Will you help?

50 **Squirrel:** We'll all help you if you just tell us what to do.

63 **Coyote:** Follow me very quietly.

68 (The animals sneak up to the Fire Beings' camp. Coyote
78 grabs a stick of fire and runs.)

85 **Chipmunk:** Look out, Coyote! The Fire Beings are
93 chasing you. Run quickly!

97 **Frog:** The Fire Beings touched the end of Coyote's tail!
107 Now the fur there is white.

Copyright © The McGraw-Hill Companies, Inc.

Name _____

113 **Squirrel:** Coyote, toss the fire to me and I'll catch it.

124   (Coyote tosses the fire to Squirrel.)

130 **Coyote:** Oh, Squirrel, you caught the fire with your
139 tail. The heat of the fire has curled your tail up over
151 your back.

153 **Chipmunk:** Squirrel, toss the fire here to me.

161   (Squirrel tosses the fire to Chipmunk.)

167 **Coyote:** Watch out, Chipmunk, a Fire Being is right
176 behind you.

178 **Frog:** The Fire Being scratched Chipmunk's back. Look
186 at the three stripes on his back. Throw the fire to me,
198 Chipmunk!

199   (Chipmunk tosses the fire to Frog. Frog is caught by a Fire
211   Being, but gets away. The fire being still holds Frog's tail.)

222 **Squirrel:** Frog, you have lost your tail!

229 **Coyote:** Here comes another Fire Being. Frog, toss the
238 fire onto Wood.

241 **Narrator:** Now Wood had fire. Coyote showed the
249 people a useful skill. He rubbed two sticks together to
259 make fire. From that day on, the people had fire.

Copyright © The McGraw-Hill Companies, Inc.

Name _____

A. Reread the passage and answer the questions.

I. What does Coyote want to do for people?

_____

_____

2. How do Coyote and the animals get fire?

_____

_____

3. What is the theme of the passage?

_____

_____

B. Work with a partner. Read the passage aloud. Pay attention to how you use your voice to show feelings. Stop after one minute. Fill out the chart.

	Words Read	–	Number of Errors	=	Words Correct Score
First Read		–		=	
Second Read		–		=	

Copyright © The McGraw-Hill Companies, Inc.

Name _____

Read the selection. Complete the Theme chart.

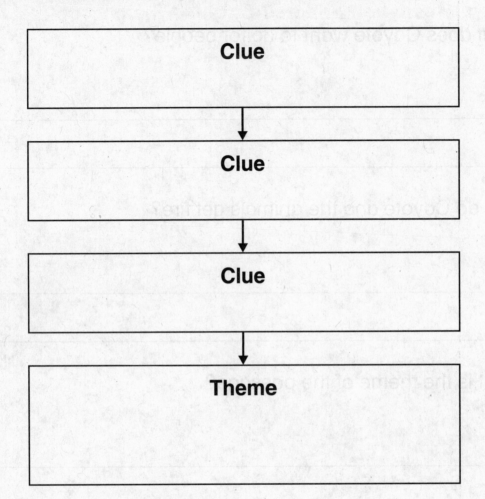

Copyright © The McGraw-Hill Companies, Inc.

Name _____

A. Read the draft model. Use the questions that follow the draft to help you add details about the characters' experiences and thoughts.

Draft Model

Sun and Moon were friends. They were nice to each other. Every day they had fun and did things together.

---

1. What might Sun and Moon think about being friends?

2. How might Sun and Moon be nice to each other?

3. What kind of fun might they have together? What are some things they might do?

B. Now revise the draft by adding details that tell about what Sun and Moon are like.

_____

_____

_____

_____

_____

_____

_____

Copyright © The McGraw-Hill Companies, Inc.

Name _____

Bear's Stumpy Tail

Fox: Bear, drop your tail in this hole in the ice. You can catch fish that way.

(Bear sits to put his tail in the ice.)

Bear: My tail is cold. I'm getting up now.

(Bear gets up. His tail snaps off. Now he has a stumpy tail.)

Answer the questions about the text.

I. How do you know this is a drama?

_____

_____

2. Why does Bear drop his tail into the hole in the ice?

_____

3. What lesson does Bear learn about Fox?

_____

Copyright © The McGraw-Hill Companies, Inc.

Name _____

> A **root word** is a word to which other word parts are added.

Read each sentence. Circle the root word in the word in bold print. Then write the meaning of the word in bold print.

1. I have a **workable** plan to take the fire.

   _____

2. Follow me very **quietly**.

   _____

3. The Fire Being **scratched** Chipmunk's back.

   _____

4. The Fire Being still **holds** Frog's tail.

   _____

5. Coyote showed the people a **useful** skill.

   _____

Copyright © The McGraw-Hill Companies, Inc.

Name _____

Reread "Coyote Brings Fire." Write about how the author uses what the characters say and do to share the theme of the story.

I. In "Coyote Brings Fire," the main characters are _____

_____

_____ .

2. Coyote wants to _____ because

_____ , so he

_____ .

3. He does this with _____

_____ .

4. The characters' words and actions are important to the author's

main message because _____

_____

_____ .

5. The theme of the story is _____

_____

_____ .

Copyright © The McGraw-Hill Companies, Inc.

Name _____

| drops | excite | outdoors | pale |

A. Choose the word that makes sense for each clue. Write the word on the line.

1. to give a strong feeling of enjoyment _____

2. not inside a building _____

3. very light in color _____

4. small amounts of liquid _____

B. Complete each sentence with a word from the box above.

5. We play _____ when the weather is nice.

6. I spilled some _____ of paint on the floor.

7. The sky was _____ blue in the early morning.

8. Squirrels playing outside the window will _____ our cat for hours.

C. Choose one vocabulary word from the box above. Write the word in a sentence of your own.

9. _____

Copyright © The McGraw-Hill Companies, Inc.

Name _____

> The letters **are**, **air**, **ear**, and **ere** can stand for the vowel sound you hear in **air**.

A. Read each row of words. Circle the word that has the same vowel sound as in *care*. Write the word on the line. Then underline the letters that spell the vowel sound.

1. peek   paint   pear   _____

2. where   wheel   when   _____

3. date   dare   dance   _____

4. chore   chair   chase   _____

5. hair   here   hard   _____

6. bark   bean   bear   _____

> When a vowel or a pair of vowels is followed by the letter ***r***, it changes the vowel sound. The vowels and the ***r*** stay in the same syllable.

B. Read each word. Draw a line between the syllables.

7. haircut   8. airport

9. turkey   10. perfect

Copyright © The McGraw-Hill Companies, Inc.

Name _____

Read the poem. Use the visualize strategy to form pictures in your mind about what happens in the poem.

The First Skate

    The temperature has been below freezing for days.
08 The pond is frozen now,
13 The ice is as smooth as glass.
20 I can ice skate outdoors
25 For the first time this winter.
31 I put on my skates and lace them up tight.
41 Then I step onto the ice and push off.
50 Right foot, left foot, right foot, left foot,
58 I glide over the ice like a bird.
66 I spin in a circle and start over again.

Copyright © The McGraw-Hill Companies, Inc.

Name _____

75	I look up,
78	Overhead, the sky curves like a blue bowl.
86	I look down,
89	Below the ice, frozen bubbles look like crystal beads.
98	As I skate, the cool breeze feels like cold fingers on my face,
111	My cheeks turn as red as apples.
118	I'm warm inside, though,
122	It feels like a fire glowing,
128	As I skate round and round the pond.
136	I keep telling myself, "One more time,"
143	Until at last it is the last time and I step off the ice,
157	Land-bound once again.

Copyright © The McGraw-Hill Companies, Inc.

Name _____

A. Reread the passage and answer the questions.

1. What was the setting of the poem?

_____

_____

2. What did the girl do?

_____

_____

3. What is the theme of the poem?

_____

_____

B. Work with a partner. Read the passage aloud. Pay attention to how you pause and group words together. Stop after one minute. Fill out the chart.

	Words Read	–	Number of Errors	=	Words Correct Score
First Read		–		=	
Second Read		–		=	

Copyright © The McGraw-Hill Companies, Inc.

Name _____

Read the selection. Complete the Theme chart.

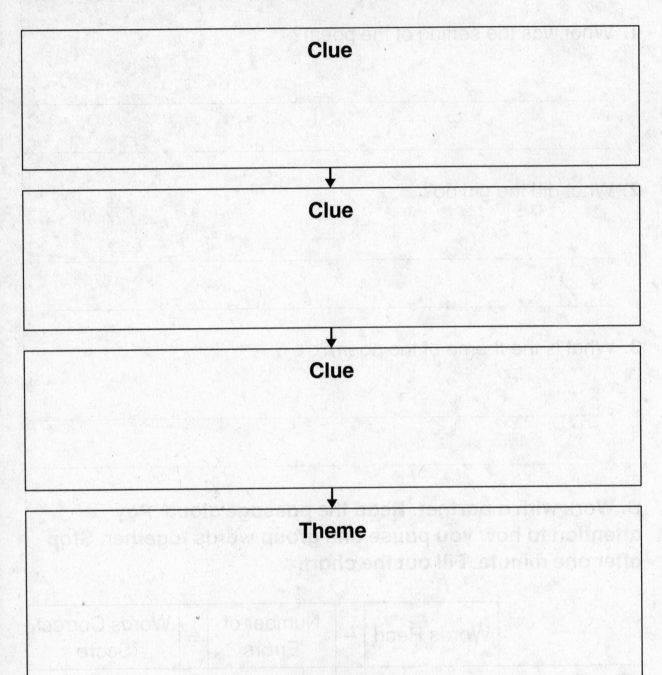

Clue

↓

Clue

↓

Clue

↓

Theme

Copyright © The McGraw-Hill Companies, Inc.

Name _____

A. Read the draft model. Use the questions that follow the draft to help you think about what sensory words you can add.

Draft Model

A butterfly flies by.
Its wings are like bright jewels.
It stops at a flower.

---

1. How does the butterfly move?

2. How do its wings look?

3. What does the flower look like? How does it smell?

B. Now revise the draft by adding sensory words about the butterfly and the flower.

_____

_____

_____

_____

Copyright © The McGraw-Hill Companies, Inc.

Name _____

A Rainy Day

The rain is pouring, pouring down,

It's so boring to stay inside.

The rain is dripping, dripping slowly.

Is it going to rain all day?

The rain is stopping, stopping now.

I can go outside and have some fun!

Answer the questions about the text.

I. How do you know this text is a poem?

_____

_____

2. What words does the poet repeat in the poem?

_____

_____

3. Why do you think the poet uses repetition?

_____

_____

Copyright © The McGraw-Hill Companies, Inc.

Name _____

> A **simile** compares two different things using the word *like* or *as*.

Read the lines from the poem. Answer the questions. Then explain what each simile means.

I. The ice is as smooth as glass.

What two things does the author compare?

_____

Meaning: _____

2. Overhead, the sky curves like a blue bowl.

What two things does the author compare?

_____

Meaning: _____

3. Below the ice, frozen bubbles look like crystal beads.

What two things does the author compare?

_____

Meaning: _____

4. My cheeks turn as red as apples.

What two things does the author compare?

_____

Meaning: _____

Copyright © The McGraw-Hill Companies, Inc.

Name _____

Reread "The First Skate." Complete the sentences by writing your opinion about the poet's word choices. Use text evidence to support your opinion.

I. In "The First Skate," the author uses words, such as _____

_____ ,

to help me understand _____

_____

_____ .

2. I like the words _____ ,

because they help me picture _____

_____

_____ .

3. I think the poet does a good job of expressing how he or she

feels about _____ ,

because _____

_____

_____ .

Copyright © The McGraw-Hill Companies, Inc.

Name _____

| champion | determined | issues | promises |
| responsibility | rights | volunteered | votes |

A. Choose the word that makes sense for each clue. Write the word on the line.

1. offered to do something _____

2. important things that people are talking about _____

3. choices given by people to elect someone _____

4. decided on something _____

5. a duty to do something _____

6. things you say you will do _____

7. a person who has won a contest _____

8. the things the law says you can do or have _____

B. Choose one vocabulary word from the box above. Write the word in a sentence of your own.

9. _____

_____

_____

Copyright © The McGraw-Hill Companies, Inc.

Name _____

> Two letters blended together can stand for one vowel
> sound. The letters **ou** and **ow** can stand for the vowel
> sound in **south** and **down**.

**A. Read the words. Circle the word that has a different vowel
sound. Write the word on the line and circle the letters that
spell the vowel sound.**

1. cloud   you   group   _____

2. blue   round   fruit   _____

3. slow   throw   cow   _____

4. pull   shout   push   _____

5. crown   snow   road   _____

> Some nouns have special plural forms. They change their
> spelling to name more than one.

B. Write the plural form for each word.

6. mouse _____   7. child _____

8. foot _____   9. man _____

Copyright © The McGraw-Hill Companies, Inc.

Name _____

Read the passage. Use the summarize strategy to tell the important events in your own words.

The Lost Kitten

00   One day, my friend Cora and I saw a homemade
10 sign posted on our street. The sign had a photo of a
22 kitten and the words, *LOST KITTEN. Please call Sally*
31 *at 555-0505 if you find my kitten, Boots.*

38   "Sally is our neighbor, Pam. She just got a new kitten
49 and now her pet is missing. It's too bad there's nothing
60 we can do," Cora said sadly.

66   I spoke up. "It's not hopeless. There is something
75 we can do! We can ask our neighbors to help look for
87 Boots."

88   We asked my dad to help with our neighborhood
97 search plan. First, we went and talked to Sally.

106   Sally explained what had happened, "I was careless
114 enough to leave the back door open. Boots slipped out
124 and ran off. And I haven't seen him since."

133   "Don't worry," I said. "We have a plan to help. Come
144 with us."

Copyright © The McGraw-Hill Companies, Inc.

Name _____

146	We all went to Mrs. Lowe's house. After Mrs. Lowe
156	heard our plan, she said, "I think that's a wonderful
166	idea. It's very thoughtful of you to help Sally find Boots.
177	I'll be happy to help with the search." She joined our
188	group.
189	At each house on the street, the answer was the same.
200	Each neighbor would gladly help search for Boots. Dad
209	divided up the neighborhood streets and told each group
218	where to look.
221	Cora and I were calling loudly, "Boots!" Suddenly we
230	heard a soft mewing sound near our feet. There was
240	Boots, crouching under a bush. I held out my hand and
251	softly called Boots's name. He came right to me and I
262	scooped up the tiny kitten.
267	When we returned Boots to Sally, she was very
276	thankful. She hugged her kitten tightly as she said,
285	"The neighborhood search plan worked. Thank you,
292	everyone!"

Copyright © The McGraw-Hill Companies, Inc.

Name _____

A. Reread the passage and answer the questions.

1. How does Cora feel about the missing kitten?

_____

_____

2. What clues help you understand Cora's point of view?

_____

_____

3. At the end of the story, what clues help you understand Sally's point of view?

_____

_____

B. Work with a partner. Read the passage aloud. Pay attention to how you raise and lower your voice. Stop after one minute. Fill out the chart.

	Words Read	–	Number of Errors	=	Words Correct Score
First Read		–		=	
Second Read		–		=	

Copyright © The McGraw-Hill Companies, Inc.

Name _____

Read the selection.
Complete the Point of View chart.

Character	Clue	Point of View

Copyright © The McGraw-Hill Companies, Inc.

Name _____

A. Read the draft model. Use the questions that follow the draft to help you think about descriptive details you can add.

> ### Draft Model
>
> Our class helped at the park. We planted a lot of things.
> I used a shovel to dig holes for trees. Other kids helped, too.
> The park looked great at the end of the day.

I. What kind of class is helping in the park?

2. What does the park look like?

3. What details might describe the kinds of things the class planted? What details might tell how the park looks at the end of the day?

B. Now revise the draft by adding descriptive details that help readers learn more about the characters, setting, and events.

_____

_____

_____

_____

Copyright © The McGraw-Hill Companies, Inc.

Name _____

Reading Volunteers

My name is Derek. The children in my second-grade class know how to read. Every Friday, we visit Ms. Snow's first-grade class. I pair up with Jack and help him practice reading. It feels good to help others.

Answer the questions about the text.

1. How can you tell that this text is realistic fiction?

_____

_____

_____

2. Who is telling the story? How do you know?

_____

_____

_____

3. How does Derek feel about helping Jack learn to read? Why do you think so?

_____

_____

_____

Copyright © The McGraw-Hill Companies, Inc.

Name _____

> To figure out a new word, look for a **suffix**, or word part, added to the end of the word.
>
> The suffix **-ly** means "in a way that is."
>
> The suffix **-ful** means "full of."
>
> The suffix **-less** means "without."

A. Underline the suffix in the word in bold print. Then write the word and its meaning.

1. "It's too bad there's nothing we can do," Cora said **sadly**.

_____

2. I was **careless** enough to leave the back door open.

_____

3. It's very **thoughtful** of you to help Sally find Boots.

_____

B. Write a word that means the same as the group of words. Your new word will end in -ful or -less.

4. without thought   **5.** full of thanks

_____   _____

Copyright © The McGraw-Hill Companies, Inc.

Name _____

Reread "The Lost Kitten." Write about how the author used point of view. Use the words and picture to help you complete the sentences below.

1. At the beginning of the story, the main characters _____

_____

_____.

2. Cora's point of view is that _____

_____

_____.

3. The narrator's point of view is that _____

_____

_____.

4. The author uses different points of view to show that _____

_____

_____.

Copyright © The McGraw-Hill Companies, Inc.

Name _____

| amused | cooperate | describe | entertained |
| imagination | interact | patient | peaceful |

Choose the word that makes sense in each blank. Then write the word on the line.

1. The book club members talk and _____ with each other when they meet.

2. The singers _____ the people at the show.

3. My friend _____ us with his funny jokes.

4. The firefighters work together, or _____, to put out the fire.

5. When there is a long line at lunch, you must be _____.

6. It is easy to relax in a _____ place.

7. Can you _____ the drawing you made?

8. You can write a good story when you use your _____.

Copyright © The McGraw-Hill Companies, Inc.

Name _____

Two letters blended together can stand for one vowel sound. The letters **oy** and **oi** can stand for the vowel sound in **boy** and **foil**.

A. Read each sentence. Circle the word with the vowel sound you hear in *boy*. Write the word on the line and circle the letters that spell the vowel sound.

I. The girl plays with a toy truck. _____

2. We'll plant seeds in the soil and watch them grow. _____

3. Dad will boil eggs in a pot on the stove. _____

4. The baby giggles with joy when she is tickled. _____

When a word ends in **-le**, the consonant before it plus the letters **le** form the last syllable. This sound in an end syllable can also be spelled **-al** or **-el**.

B. Read each word. Draw a line between the syllables. Write each syllable on the line.

I. needle _____ _____

2. bagel _____ _____

3. local _____ _____

4. puzzle _____ _____

Copyright © The McGraw-Hill Companies, Inc.

Name _____

Read the passage. Use the summarize strategy to tell the important events in your own words.

The Class Play

00   Mr. Webb's class was going to put on a play for the
12   school. They chose to act out *Henny Penny.*

20   "There are six actors in this play," said Mr. Webb.
30   "We'll need painters for the sets. We'll need helpers with
40   the lights and music. There will be a job for everyone."

51   The next day, the class read the play together. Luz
61   said, "I'm going to play the part of Henny Penny. That's
72   the most important part."

76   "No, I want to play that part," said Jade.

85   "I think I would be the best Henny Penny," chimed in
96   Stacy.

97   Before the talk could get out of hand, Mr. Webb spoke
108   up. "We have to be fair. We will have a try-out and I
122   will be the judge."

Copyright © The McGraw-Hill Companies, Inc.

Name _____

126   Mr. Webb explained that children who wanted to act
135 in the play should practice the lines. Then Mr. Webb
145 would decide who was best for each part.

153   The class agreed that this was fair. They knew if they
164 all pulled together, they could put on a great play.

174   Luz made up her mind that she wanted to play Henny
185 Penny. She practiced her lines over and over. She knew
195 the lines by heart.

199   At the try-out, three children read the part of Henny
210 Penny. Other children tried out for the rest of the parts.
221 Mr. Webb clapped for each child. Then he said, "Luz,
231 you will play Henny Penny. Here is a list of the other
243 parts and jobs for all."

248   The class worked hard on their play. Everyone at
257 school said it was a big hit!

Copyright © The McGraw-Hill Companies, Inc.

Name _____

A. Reread the passage and answer the questions.

1. What is Luz's point of view about who should play the part of Henny Penny?

_____

_____

2. What is Stacy's point of view about who should play the part of Henny Penny?

_____

_____

3. What is Mr. Webb's point of view about who should play the part of Henny Penny?

_____

_____

B. Work with a partner. Read the passage aloud.
Pay attention to how you use your voice to show feelings.
Stop after one minute. Fill out the chart.

	Words Read	–	Number of Errors	=	Words Correct Score
First Read		–		=	
Second Read		–		=	

Copyright © The McGraw-Hill Companies, Inc.

Name _____

Read the selection.
Complete the Point of View chart.

Character	Clue	Point of View

Copyright © The McGraw-Hill Companies, Inc.

Name _____

A. Read the draft model. Use the questions that follow the draft to help you think about using sentences of different lengths.

> **Draft Model**
>
> Jake had to do a project. It was for science. He and his friends worked together. It made the work go faster. They built a toy rocket ship. Soon they were done.

1. Which sentences could you make longer?

2. Which sentences could you combine?

3. How can you make the sentences flow from one to the next?

B. Now revise the draft by writing sentences of different lengths.

_____

_____

_____

_____

_____

_____

Copyright © The McGraw-Hill Companies, Inc.

Name _____

Sharing the Class Pet

Marta's class has a pet rabbit. On Friday, everyone wants to take the rabbit home. Mrs. Jones writes the children's names on papers and mixes them up. She will pick a name to see who takes the rabbit home today.

Answer the questions about the text.

1. How do you know that this text is fiction?

_____

_____

2. What is the problem?

_____

_____

3. What is the solution?

_____

_____

Copyright © The McGraw-Hill Companies, Inc.

Name _____

> An **idiom** is a word or a phrase that has a different meaning than the real meaning of the words.

**Read each sentence. Look at the idiom in bold print.
Write the meaning of the idiom.**

1. Before the talk could **get out of hand**, Mr. Webb spoke up.

_____

2. They knew if they all **pulled together**, they could put on a great play.

_____

3. Luz **made up her mind** that she wanted to play Henny Penny.

_____

4. She **knew the lines by heart**.

_____

5. Everyone at school said **it was a big hit**!

_____

Copyright © The McGraw-Hill Companies, Inc.

Name _____

Reread "The Class Play." Write about how the author used point of view. Use the words and picture to help you complete the sentences below.

1. At the beginning of the story, Luz's point of view is that _____

_____

_____.

2. One clue that the author gives is that Luz said, _____

_____

_____.

3. Toward the end of the story, Luz's point of view is that _____

_____

_____.

4. One clue that the author gives is _____

_____

_____.

5. Understanding Luz's point of view helps me _____

_____

_____.

Copyright © The McGraw-Hill Companies, Inc.

Name _____

agree	challenging	discover	heroes
interest	perform	succeed	study

Choose the word that makes sense in each blank. Then write the word on the line.

1. My aunt has an _____ in learning to knit.

2. The boy found it _____ to complete the puzzle.

3. Do you _____ or disagree with my idea?

4. You should _____ the spelling words before taking the test.

5. The _____ helped many people to safety.

6. I would like to _____ a new star in the sky.

7. Five actors _____ in a play on stage.

8. You can _____ at playing the piano with lots of practice.

Copyright © The McGraw-Hill Companies, Inc.

Name _____

> The letters **oo**, **u_e**, **u**, **ew**, **ue**, and **ui** can stand for the
> vowel sound you hear in the words **moon**, **tune**, **flu**, **chew**,
> **blue**, and **suit**. The letters **oo**, **ou**, and **u** can also stand for
> the vowel sound you hear in **look**, **would**, and **push**.

**A. Write each word in the box to match the word in bold print
with the same vowel sound.**

> | drew | goose | could | full |
> |------|-------|-------|------|
> | flute | good | true | should |

pool

1. _____

2. _____

3. _____

4. _____

book

5. _____

6. _____

7. _____

8. _____

> A contraction is a short way to write two words. The
> apostrophe takes the place of the letter *o* in the word **not**.

B. Write the contraction for each pair of words.

9. should not _____

10. has not _____

11. would not _____

12. could not _____

Copyright © The McGraw-Hill Companies, Inc.

Name _____

Read the passage. Use the summarize strategy to tell the important events in your own words.

Dr. Elizabeth Blackwell

00   Today many women are **doctors**, but that was
08 not always true. Many years ago, only men could be
18 doctors. Elizabeth Blackwell changed that.

23 **Early Life**

25   Elizabeth Blackwell was born in England in 1821. Her
34 family moved to America when Elizabeth was eleven.
42 When she got older, she became a teacher. In that time,
53 teaching was a common occupation, or job, for women.

62 **Becoming a Doctor**

65   Then one of Elizabeth's friends got very ill. She wanted
75 sick people to have less pain and discomfort. Elizabeth
84 started thinking about ways to help people like her
93 friend. She wanted to become a doctor.

Copyright © The McGraw-Hill Companies, Inc.

Name _____

100   Elizabeth talked to men doctors who told her that
109 women could not go to **medical school**. Elizabeth did not
119 agree or accept that. She tried to get into a number of
131 medical schools. She did not give up.

138   At last, she was allowed to study at a school in New
150 York. Elizabeth studied and learned medicine for two
158 years. In 1849, she became the first woman doctor in
168 America.

169   A few years later, Elizabeth opened her own medical
178 office in New York City. She asked two other women
188 doctors to join her **practice**. One of these doctors was
198 her sister, Emily. The doctors took care of sick women
208 and children. They also ran a school to train, or teach,
219 other women as doctors.

223   Elizabeth Blackwell helped people her whole life. She
231 opened the door for women doctors.

Copyright © The McGraw-Hill Companies, Inc.

Name _____

A. Reread the passage and answer the questions.

I. What happened first in Elizabeth Blackwell's life?

_____

_____

2. What happened next?

_____

_____

3. What happened last?

_____

_____

B. Work with a partner. Read the passage aloud. Pay attention to how you pause and group words together. Stop after one minute. Fill out the chart.

	Words Read	–	Number of Errors	=	Words Correct Score
First Read		–		=	
Second Read		–		=	

Copyright © The McGraw-Hill Companies, Inc.

Name _____

Read the selection. Complete the Sequence chart.

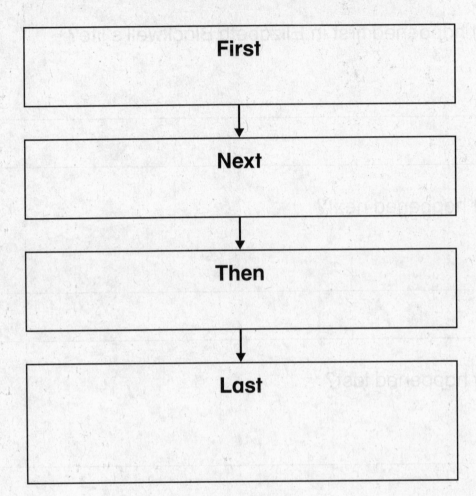

First

↓

Next

↓

Then

↓

Last

Copyright © The McGraw-Hill Companies, Inc.

Name _____

A. Read the draft model. Use the questions that follow the draft to help you think about the correct sequence of events.

> ### Draft Model
>
> Doug grew up in the city. When Doug got older, he helped out at the library. Today, he helps students with their reading. He liked to read when he was a boy.

I. What happens first in Doug's life?

2. What happens next?

3. What does Doug do today?

B. Now revise the draft by including events in the correct sequence in which they happened in Doug's life.

_____

_____

_____

_____

_____

Copyright © The McGraw-Hill Companies, Inc.

Name _____

Jesse Owens

In junior high school, Jesse Owens joined the track team. He set **records** in running. Later, at age 22, Jesse won races in the **Olympics**. He proved that everyone can do great things.

1913	1928	1936	1976
Jesse Owens is born	His athletic career began during junior high school	He wins 4 Olympic gold medals	He wins the U.S. Medal of Freedom

Answer the questions about the text.

1. How do you know this is a biography?

_____

2. Why are the words **records** and **Olympics** in bold print?

_____

3. What information does the time line help you learn?

_____

4. What happened to Jesse Owens in 1936?

_____

Copyright © The McGraw-Hill Companies, Inc.

Name _____

> **Synonyms** are words that have almost the same meaning.

Read each sentence. Write the two words that are synonyms.

I. In that time, teaching was a common occupation, or job, for women.

_____   _____

2. She wanted sick people to have less pain and discomfort.

_____   _____

3. Elizabeth did not agree or accept that.

_____   _____

4. Elizabeth studied and learned medicine for two years.

_____   _____

5. They also ran a school to train, or teach, other women as doctors.

_____   _____

Copyright © The McGraw-Hill Companies, Inc.

Name _____

Reread "Dr. Elizabeth Blackwell." Write your opinion about how the author used sequence. Use the words and picture to help you complete the sentences below.

I. In the selection, the author did a good job of using sequence to

_____

because _____

_____ .

2. The first event that the author writes about is _____

_____

_____ .

3. One of the next events the author writes about is _____

_____

_____ .

4. The last event the author writes about is _____ .

_____

_____ .

5. Reading the events in sequence helps me _____

_____

_____ .

Copyright © The McGraw-Hill Companies, Inc.

Name _____

curious	distance	Earth resources	enormous
gently	proudly	rarely	supply

Read the story. Choose words from the box to complete the sentences. Then write the answers on the lines.

Sam was eager to learn, or _____ about

coal. He traveled quite a _____ to the library. There

he found an _____ book. It was about _____.

The book was _____ used, so it looked new. Sam did

not want to rip the pages, so he turned them _____.

He learned that there is a _____ of coal underground.

Sam _____ reported all he had learned about coal to

his class.

Copyright © The McGraw-Hill Companies, Inc.

Name _____

> The letters **a**, **aw**, **au**, **augh**, **al**, and **ough** can stand for the vowel sound you hear in **call**, **dawn**, **sauce**, **caught**, **salt**, and **thought**.

A. Read each word. Circle the word that has the same vowel sound as the first word. Write it on the line. Underline the letters that spell the vowel sound.

1. **yawn**   bank   fault   _____

2. **cause**   hawk   rail   _____

3. **hall**   fought   last   _____

4. **walk**   sale   tall   _____

5. **taught**   day   chalk   _____

> In a long word, the letters that make up a vowel team stay together in the same syllable.

B. Draw a line to divide each word into syllables. Circle the vowel team.

6. yellow

7. awful

8. pointer

9. caution

Copyright © The McGraw-Hill Companies, Inc.

Name _____

Read the passage. Use the make predictions strategy to tell what you think might happen next.

The Recycling Contest

00   Ms. Hines was the principal at Grover School. Each
09 day, she saw that students threw away sheets and sheets
19 of paper. She called a meeting to talk about recycling.

29   Ms. Hines explained why recycling was important.
36 She ended her speech this way, "Let's help save the
46 Earth. If we all pitch in, we can make a difference."

57   The students cheered and went back to their rooms.
66 The next few days, Ms. Hines watched the students.
75 They were not recycling! Ms. Hines decided to try
84 another plan.

86   "Grover School is having a contest," she told the
95 students. "The class that recycles the most paper in one
105 week will win a prize. The contest begins tomorrow."

114   "Our class can win," said Eric. He was in second
124 grade.

125   His teacher, Mrs. Park, said, "Let's try our best."

Copyright © The McGraw-Hill Companies, Inc.

Name _____

134   Ms. Hines gave each class a recycling bin. She made a
145 big wall chart. Each time a class filled a bin with paper,
157 they emptied it into a giant container. Ms. Hines kept
167 track of the paper on her chart.

174   Eric reminded all his classmates to recycle. If he saw
184 someone throwing away some paper, Eric called, "Put
192 that paper in the bin." He never forgot to recycle.

202   At the end of the week, Ms. Hines called another
212 meeting. She held up the recycling chart. Eric's class had
222 won the contest!

225   "This is your prize," she said. "You get an extra ten
236 minutes outside at recess for one week. You can enjoy
246 the Earth that you are helping to save!"

Copyright © The McGraw-Hill Companies, Inc.

Name _____

A. Reread the passage and answer the questions.

1. What is the problem in the passage?

_____

_____

2. What is one step that Ms. Hines takes to solve the problem?

_____

_____

3. What is the solution to the problem?

_____

_____

B. Work with a partner. Read the passage aloud. Pay attention to how you raise and lower your voice. Stop after one minute. Fill out the chart.

	Words Read	−	Number of Errors	=	Words Correct Score
First Read		−		=	
Second Read		−		=	

Copyright © The McGraw-Hill Companies, Inc.

Name _____

Read the selection. Complete the Problem and Solution chart.

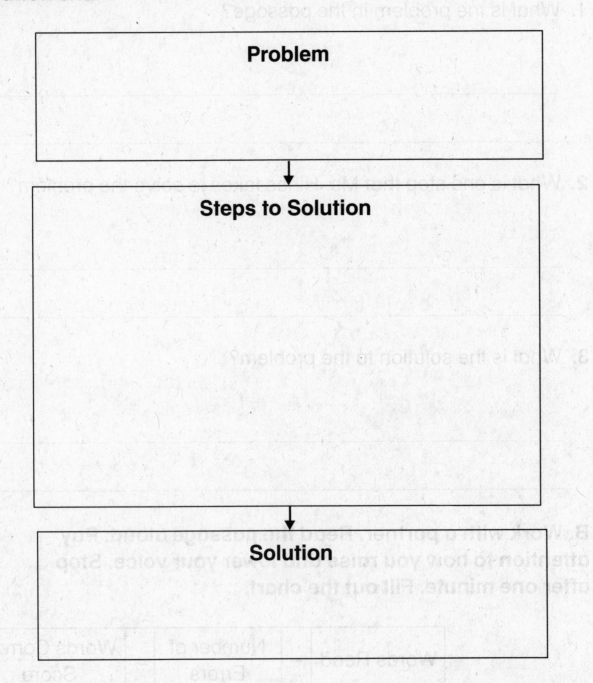

Problem

Steps to Solution

Solution

Copyright © The McGraw-Hill Companies, Inc.

Name _____

A. Read the draft model. Use the questions that follow the draft to help you add linking words to connect ideas.

> **Draft Model**
>
> My family I went to the park for a picnic. We sat in one area. We were not happy. People had left a lot of trash there. We moved to another area. We were happy.

1. Why does the family move from the first area?

2. Why is the family happy with the second area?

3. What are some words you can use to show how ideas are connected?

B. Now revise the draft by adding words that connect ideas and help readers understand why things happen.

_____
_____
_____
_____
_____
_____

Copyright © The McGraw-Hill Companies, Inc.

Name _____

Let's Ride!

"Let's drive to the park," said Mom.

Joan said, "Driving cars can harm the Earth. Let's ride our bikes there instead."

Mom liked Joan's plan for protecting the Earth.

Answer the questions about the text.

1. How do you know this text is fiction?

_____

_____

2. What is Mom's dialogue in the story?

_____

_____

3. What is the problem?

_____

4. What is the solution?

_____

Copyright © The McGraw-Hill Companies, Inc.

Name _____

Vocabulary Strategy: **Homophones**

> **Homophones** are words that sound the same but have different spellings and meanings.

Read each sentence. Choose the definition that fits the homophone in bold print. Write it on the line.

1. Each day, she saw that students **threw** away sheets and sheets of paper.

   went from one side to another   tossed

   _____

2. The students cheered and went back **to** their rooms.

   in the direction of   the number after one

   _____

3. The class that recycles the most paper in one **week** will win a prize.

   seven days   not strong

   _____

4. She **made** a big wall chart.

   helper   created

   _____

Name _____

Reread "The Recycling Contest." Write about how the author used problem and solution. Use the words and picture to help you complete the sentences below.

I. The problem the author presented at the beginning of the story was

_____

_____

_____

_____ .

2. The steps the characters took to solve the problem are

_____

_____

_____

_____ .

3. The steps to the solution are in sequence, or time order, because

_____

_____

_____

_____ .

Copyright © The McGraw-Hill Companies, Inc.

Name _____

exclaimed	finally	form	history
public	rules	united	writers

Read the story. Choose words from the box to complete the sentences. Then write the answers on the lines.

Throughout its long _____, Mr. Finch's town had

never had a library. He wanted everyone to be able to read

books by great _____. Mr. Finch _____,

"We need a _____ library that everyone can use!"

Mr. Finch followed the town's strict _____. He took

his time to make, or _____, a group. The people in the

group were joined, or _____, in their cause. After much

work, Mr. Finch and his group _____ got a library built

for their town!

Copyright © The McGraw-Hill Companies, Inc.

Name _____

> The letters **ea** can stand for the vowel sound you hear in **bread**.
> The letters **ou** can stand for the vowel sound you hear in **touch**.
> The letter **y** can stand for the vowel sound you hear in **myth**.

A. Read each word. Circle the word that has the same vowel sound as the first word. Write it on the line. Underline the letters that spell the vowel sound.

1. **rough**   double   count   _____

2. **thread**   steak   wealth   _____

3. **myth**   find   gym   _____

4. **head**   breath   please   _____

> When two words begin with the same letter, you can look at the second letter to put the word in alphabetical order.

B. Read the words in each row. Write them in alphabetical order.

5. after, apple, ahead   _____

6. couple, class, crumb   _____

7. swim, saddle, south   _____

8. lead, lucky, land   _____

Copyright © The McGraw-Hill Companies, Inc.

Name _____

Read the passage. Use the make predictions strategy to tell what you think you might read about.

Sports Rules

Rules are important in sports. Rules tell players how
09 to play a game. They tell how to score points. They tell
21 how a game is won. They also tell players what they
32 can and cannot do. All players in a game must agree to
44 the same rules. Sometimes a player breaks a rule. Then
54 he or she may not be allowed to play for all or part of
68 the game.

70 **Basketball Rules**

72 Have you ever played basketball? If not, the name
81 "basketball" gives you a clue about some of the rules.
91 Basketball is played with a ball on a basketball court.
101 Players score points by throwing the ball through a
110 basket, or hoop.

113 There are rules about how to move the ball in
123 basketball. Players must dribble, or bounce, the ball.
131 They may also pass, or throw, the ball to another player.
142 They may not hold the ball and run with it. This would
154 not allow other players a chance to get the ball.

Copyright © The McGraw-Hill Companies, Inc.

Name _____

Sport	Number of Players	Moving the Ball	Scoring
baseball	9	throw and hit	cross home plate for one run
basketball	5	dribble and pass	shoot basket for points

164 **Baseball Rules**

166   Baseball rules are different from basketball rules. The
174 pitcher from one team throws a ball to the batter on the
186 other team. The batter gets three chances to hit the ball
197 with a bat. Sometimes the batter misses. This is called
207 a strike. After three strikes, the batter is out. Then it is
219 another batter's turn.

222   When the batter hits the ball, he or she runs around
233 four bases. The last base is home plate. The batter
243 crosses home plate to score a run. The other team tries
254 to get the batter out. They can tag the batter with the
266 ball. Then the batter cannot score a run.

274   Without rules, sports would be confusing. No one
282 would know the way to play a game. Rules make every
293 player a good sport!

Copyright © The McGraw-Hill Companies, Inc.

Name _____

A. Reread the passage and answer the questions.

I. Why are rules important in sports?

_____

_____

2. What happens when a basketball player shoots the ball through the hoop?

_____

_____

3. What happens when a batter in baseball gets three strikes?

_____

_____

B. Work with a partner. Read the passage aloud. Pay attention to pronunciation. Stop after one minute. Fill out the chart.

	Words Read	–	Number of Errors	=	Words Correct Score
First Read		–		=	
Second Read		–		=	

Copyright © The McGraw-Hill Companies, Inc.

Name _____

Read the selection. Complete the Cause and Effect chart.

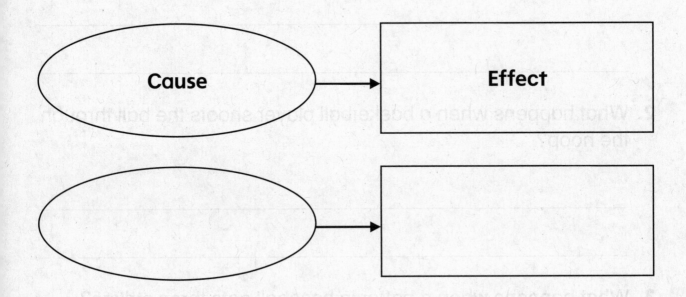

Copyright © The McGraw-Hill Companies, Inc.

Name _____

A. Read the draft model. Use the questions that follow the draft to help you think about how to make the writing more informal.

Draft Model

We have a great school because everyone follows the rules! Here are some of the rules. Walk in the halls. Do not run. Respect teachers and students. Enjoy learning every day.

I. Where could you use contractions?

2. Where could you add exclamations?

3. Which sentences could you change to make the writing sound more like natural speaking?

B. Now revise the draft by using a more informal voice, one that sounds like natural speaking.

_____

_____

_____

_____

_____

Copyright © The McGraw-Hill Companies, Inc.

Name _____

Safety Rules

Here are some ways to stay safe while having fun. When you ride a bike, wear a helmet. Wear a helmet and pads when you skateboard. If you take a trip in the car, always wear a seat belt.

Activity	Safety Equipment
bike ride	
skateboarding	
boat ride	
car ride	

Answer the questions about the text.

1. How do you know this is expository text?

_____

2. What information can you learn from the chart?

_____

3. What should someone wear when going for a boat ride?

_____

Copyright © The McGraw-Hill Companies, Inc.

Name _____

> **Multiple-meaning words** have more than one meaning. Use other words in the sentence to figure out which meaning is being used.

Read each sentence. Choose the meaning of the word in bold print. Write it on the line.

1. **Rules** are important in sports.

   things that tell how to behave   make laws and decide things

   _____

2. Rules tell players how to **play** a game.

   a story that is acted out   to take part in a sports game

   _____

3. Basketball is played with a ball on a basketball **court**.

   the place where a ruler lives   an area used for playing a sport

   _____

4. Players must **dribble**, or bounce, the ball.

   to move a ball by bouncing   to spill drops of liquid

   _____

5. The pitcher throws a ball to the **batter** on the other team.

   a mixture used in cooking   a player who hits a baseball

   _____

Copyright © The McGraw-Hill Companies, Inc.

Name _____

Reread "Sports Rules." Write about how the author used cause and effect. Use the words and chart to help you complete the sentences below.

I. In the selection, the author explains _____

_____

_____

_____ .

2. The effect of a player breaking a rule is _____

_____

_____

_____ .

3. The author used cause and effect to help readers understand

_____

_____

_____

_____ .

Copyright © The McGraw-Hill Companies, Inc.

Name _____

| appeared | crops | develop | edge |
| golden | rustled | shining | stages |

Read the story. Choose words from the box to complete the sentences. Then write the answers on the lines.

The farmer had tried growing different

_____, but each one failed. "I must

_____ new seeds," thought the farmer. So this

is what he did. He planted different kinds of seeds and

recorded their _____ of growth.

Then the farmer chose the best seeds and planted

them in his fields. Soon green sprouts _____.

After many weeks, the farmer saw the _____

wheat growing. It grew fast in the _____ sun.

The wheat _____ in the wind. The farmer

walked along the _____ of his fields, proud of

what he had done.

Copyright © The McGraw-Hill Companies, Inc.

Name _____

> A syllable must always have a vowel. When a syllable ends in a vowel, it is an **open syllable** and usually has a long vowel sound, as in *frozen*, *fro / zen*. When a syllable ends in a consonant, it is a **closed syllable** and usually has a short vowel sound, as in *kitten*, *kit / ten*.

A. Draw a line between the syllables in each word. Then write each syllable.

1. magnet _____ _____

2. robot _____ _____

3. hidden _____ _____

4. pencil _____ _____

5. crayon _____ _____

> A **compound word** is a word that is made up of two smaller words.

B. Read each sentence. Circle the compound word. Write its meaning.

6. The student wrote in his notebook. _____

7. The girl painted her bedroom. _____

8. Plants need water and sunlight. _____

Copyright © The McGraw-Hill Companies, Inc.

Name _____

Read the passage. Use the reread strategy to check your understanding of story events.

The Contest of Athens

Long ago, the city of Athens needed a patron,
9   someone to watch over the city. There were two great
19 beings who wished to be the patron. One was Poseidon,
29 who ruled the seas. The other was Athena, who had
39 great wisdom.

41   The king of Athens had to select one of these two. So
53 he asked each one to give a valuable and important gift
64 to Athens.

66   "Your gift must be something useful for the city," said
76 the king.

78   It was Poseidon's turn first. He hit the ground with his
89 spear, the long-handled blade he always carried. From
98 the ground, a well appeared. Water began to flow.

107   The king hurried to the well to taste the water. He
118 found that the water was as salty as the sea.

128   "This will not do as a gift to Athens," he said.

Copyright © The McGraw-Hill Companies, Inc.

Name _____

139	Next, it was Athena's turn. She also hit the ground
149	with her spear. In that spot, she buried an olive branch
160	in the ground to make an olive tree. The olive tree
171	would give the people of Athens food, oil, and wood.
181	The king was very happy with Athena's fine gift. He
191	stated, "Because you have given us this olive tree, I will
202	make you the patron of Athens."
208	Athena was pleased, but Poseidon was dejected at
216	losing the contest. He flooded the land with seawater.
225	Once he calmed down, he drained the floodwater away.

Copyright © The McGraw-Hill Companies, Inc.

Name _____

A. Reread the passage and answer the questions.

I. What was Poseidon's gift to Athens? How did the king feel about Poseidon's gift?

_____

_____

2. What was Athena's gift to Athens? How did the king feel about Athena's gift?

_____

_____

3. What is the theme of the passage?

_____

_____

B. Work with a partner. Read the passage aloud. Pay attention to how you use your voice to show feelings. Stop after one minute. Fill out the chart.

	Words Read	−	Number of Errors	=	Words Correct Score
First Read		−		=	
Second Read		−		=	

Copyright © The McGraw-Hill Companies, Inc.

Name _____

Read the selection. Complete the Theme chart.

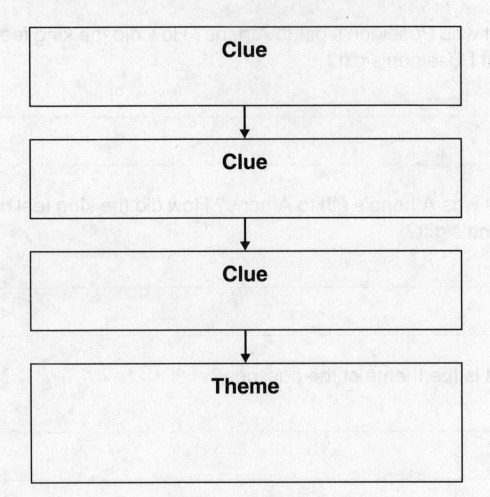

Clue

↓

Clue

↓

Clue

↓

Theme

Copyright © The McGraw-Hill Companies, Inc.

Name _____

A. Read the draft model. Use the questions that follow the draft to help you think about a strong opening you can add.

> ### Draft Model
>
> Once there was a flower. It was in a forest. It needed rain.

I. What does the flower look like? How does it feel and act?

2. What does the forest look like?

3. What problem might the flower have?

B. Now revise the draft by writing a strong opening that tells about the character, the setting, and a problem.

_____

_____

_____

_____

_____

_____

_____

Copyright © The McGraw-Hill Companies, Inc.

Name _____

Clytie and Apollo

Apollo was the ruler of the sun. Clytie loved to watch Apollo as he moved across the sky. She watched him so often that she became a sunflower. Even today sunflowers turn to the sun.

Answer the questions about the text.

I. How do you know that this text is a myth?

_____

_____

2. Who is Apollo?

_____

3. Why does Clytie look up at the sky?

_____

4. What does the myth explain?

_____

_____

Copyright © The McGraw-Hill Companies, Inc.

> Look at this example of **context clues** in a sentence. The underlined words help explain what *select* means.
>
> The king of Athens had to **select** <u>one of these two</u>.

Read each sentence. Write the meaning of the word in bold print. Underline the context clues in the sentence that helped you.

1. Long ago, the city of Athens needed a **patron**, someone to watch over the city.

    _____

2. So he asked each one to give a **valuable** and important gift to Athens.

    _____

3. He hit the ground with his **spear**, the long-handled blade he always carried.

    _____

4. In that spot, she **buried** an olive branch in the ground to make an olive tree.

    _____

5. Athena was pleased, but Poseidon was **dejected** at losing the contest.

    _____

Copyright © The McGraw-Hill Companies, Inc.

Name _____

Reread "The Contest of Athens." Write about how the author used clues to support the theme of the text. Use the words and picture to help you complete the sentences below.

1. A clue to the theme of the story is that _____

_____

_____

2. Another clue the author includes is that _____

_____

_____

3. After Athena was chosen to be the patron of Athens, Poseidon

_____

_____

4. The theme of the story is _____

_____

_____

Copyright © The McGraw-Hill Companies, Inc.

Name _____

| electricity | energy | flows | haul |
| power | silent | solar | underground |

Use what you know about the words in the sentences to choose the word that makes sense in each blank. Then write the word on the line.

1. Will you help me _____ these bags of leaves to the shed?

2. We can get _____ from eating healthful foods.

3. The classroom was _____ during the test.

4. Moving water has the _____ to move rocks.

5. Worms make their home _____.

6. A river _____ through the middle of the city.

7. The man set up a _____ panel on the roof of his house to collect the sun's rays.

8. We cannot turn on a light without _____.

Copyright © The McGraw-Hill Companies, Inc.

Name _____

A syllable that has the **vowel consonant e** pattern often has the long vowel sound. In the word *excite*, the syllable *cite* has the long *i* sound.

A. Circle four words in the box that have a vowel consonant *e* syllable. Then write the syllables in each circled word.

compete	tiger	replace	zebra	arrive	pollute

1. _____ _____   2. _____ _____

3. _____ _____   4. _____ _____

A **prefix** is added to the beginning of a word. A **suffix** is added to the end of a word.

Prefixes   **Suffixes**
re- = "again"   *-ful* = "full of"
un- and *dis-* = "not" or "opposite of"   *-less* = "without"

B. Read each clue. Write a word with a prefix or a suffix to match each clue.

5. full of joy _____   6. not wise _____

7. without fear _____   8. visit again _____

9. the opposite of approve _____

Copyright © The McGraw-Hill Companies, Inc.

Name _____

Read the passage. Use the reread strategy to check your understanding of new information or difficult facts.

Ocean Energy

We use energy every day to do work. With energy, we
11 can turn on a light, heat a home, cook food, and run a
24 computer. Much of our energy comes from coal, oil, and
34 gas. Some of our energy comes from the sun and the
45 wind. One day, we might even get our energy from the
56 ocean.

57 Yes, energy can come from the ocean. There are not
67 many ocean power plants right now. But the ocean is a
78 big source of energy.

82 Tidal Energy

84 The ocean has high and low tides. This means the
94 water rises and falls every twelve hours. This tidal
103 energy can be used to make power.

110 When high tide flows in to shore, the water is trapped
121 behind a dam. The water is stored in a large pool. When
133 low tide occurs, the water behind the dam is let out.
144 The rushing water runs a machine inside the dam. The
154 machine makes electricity.

Copyright © The McGraw-Hill Companies, Inc.

Name _____

157 **Ocean Wave Energy**

160   The water in the ocean is always moving. The
169 movement of ocean waves can run a machine built to
179 produce power. The waves move up and down inside the
189 machine. They spin parts of the machine. The machine
198 makes electricity.

200 **Heat Energy**

202   The water temperature on the ocean's surface is
210 warmer than below. That's because the sun heats the
219 water on top. Deep below the surface, the water is very
230 cold.

231   This temperature difference creates heat energy. A
238 power plant uses this heat energy to make electricity.

247   The ocean is a giant source of energy. Maybe one day
258 the ocean will power the world.

Copyright © The McGraw-Hill Companies, Inc.

Name _____

A. Reread the passage and answer the questions.

1. What is this passage about?

_____

_____

2. What is one fact that the author includes about ocean energy?

_____

_____

3. What is another fact that the author includes about ocean energy?

_____

_____

4. What is the author's purpose for writing this passage?

_____

B. Work with a partner. Read the passage aloud. Pay attention to how you use intonation. Stop after one minute. Fill out the chart.

	Words Read	−	Number of Errors	=	Words Correct Score
First Read		−		=	
Second Read		−		=	

Copyright © The McGraw-Hill Companies, Inc.

Name _____

Read the selection. Complete the Author's Purpose chart.

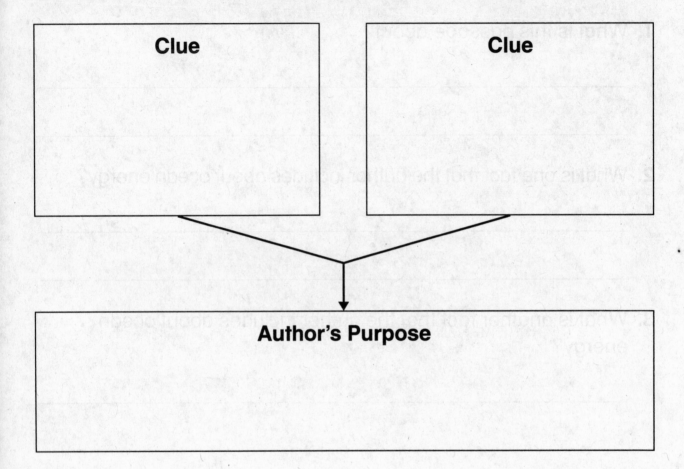

Copyright © The McGraw-Hill Companies, Inc.

Name _____

A. Read the draft model. Use the questions that follow the draft to help you think about adding content words.

Draft Model

A radio needs something to make it work. It can run on electricity. It can also run on a battery. Some radios have a sun panel to charge the battery.

I. What content words can you add to tell about a radio?

2. What content words can you add to tell about electricity?

3. What content words can you add to tell about a battery?

B. Now revise the draft by adding content words that are related to radios, electricity, and batteries.

_____

_____

_____

_____

_____

_____

_____

Copyright © The McGraw-Hill Companies, Inc.

Name _____

Each Can Counts

Recycling a can means that the same material can be used again. Energy is not wasted getting new materials to make a new can. The energy saved by recycling one can may run a TV for three hours.

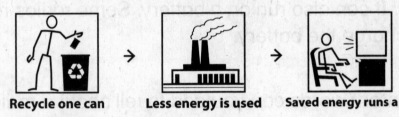

Recycle one can   **Less energy is used**   **Saved energy runs a TV**

Answer the questions about the text.

I. How do you know this is expository text?

_____

_____

2. Why is it important to recycle cans?

_____

3. What information does the diagram show?

_____

_____

4. What action does the first label tell about?

_____

_____

Copyright © The McGraw-Hill Companies, Inc.

Name _____

Look at this example of **context clues** in a paragraph. The underlined words help explain what *energy* means.

We use **energy** every day to <u>do work</u>. With energy, we can <u>turn on a light</u>, <u>heat a home</u>, <u>cook food</u>, and <u>run a computer</u>.

Read each paragraph. Write the meaning of the word in bold print. Underline the context clues that helped you.

1. Yes, energy can come from the ocean. There are not many ocean power plants right now. But the ocean is a big **source** of energy.

_____

2. The ocean has high and low **tides**. This means the water rises and falls every twelve hours. This tidal energy can be used to make power.

_____

3. The movement of ocean waves can run a machine built to produce power. The waves move up and down inside the machine. They spin parts of the machine. The machine makes **electricity**.

_____

4. The water temperature on the ocean's **surface** is warmer than below. That's because the sun heats the water on top. Deep below the surface, the water is very cold.

_____

Copyright © The McGraw-Hill Companies, Inc.

Name _____

Reread "Ocean Energy." Write about how the author used clues and text features to tell the purpose for writing the text. Use the words and picture to complete the sentences.

I. The author's purpose for writing this selection is _____

_____

_____.

2. A clue to the author's purpose is _____

_____

_____.

3. Another clue to the author's purpose is _____

_____

_____.

4. A picture is included in the text to help the reader _____

_____

_____.

Copyright © The McGraw-Hill Companies, Inc.

Name _____

| exploration | important | machines | prepare |
| repair | result | scientific | teamwork |

Choose the word that makes sense in each blank. Then write the word on the line.

1. Lawn mowers are _____ that make it easier to cut grass.

2. She will study the honeybees in a _____ way.

3. I need to _____ this broken computer.

4. It's _____ to listen when someone speaks to you.

5. The scientists planned for a rain forest _____.

6. The _____ of the heavy rain was a flood.

7. How will you _____ for your camping trip?

8. Use _____ to do a job that is too big for one person.

Copyright © The McGraw-Hill Companies, Inc.

Name _____

> When a word ends in a consonant plus **-le**, **-el**, or **-al**, the consonant and the letters *-le, -el,* or *-al* often make the last syllable in the word, as in **needle**, **bagel**, and **local**.

A. Draw a line between the syllables in each word. Then write each syllable.

1. hazel   _____ · _____

2. purple   _____ _____

3. sandal   _____ _____

4. cable   _____ _____

> A **contraction** is used to combine two words. An apostrophe takes the place of a missing letter or letters: **do not = don't**.
>
> A **possessive noun** has an apostrophe and the letter *s* to show ownership: **Mom's car**.

B. Read each sentence. Look at the underlined word. If it is a contraction, write the two words. If it is a possessive noun, write to tell who or what owns or has what.

5. The boy <u>couldn't</u> get his toy robot to work.

_____

6. The <u>boy's</u> father put in a new battery.

_____

Copyright © The McGraw-Hill Companies, Inc.

Name _____

Read the passage. Use the summarize strategy to tell the important ideas in your own words.

An Antarctic Team

	Teams of people explore places all over the globe.
09	Why do they work in teams? Each person has special
19	skills that help out the whole team.
26	
	The Antarctic is an incredible place to explore. Each
35	year, teams travel there to study the region. Each team
45	member has an important job to do.
52	
	One of the first jobs is to set up a research station,
65	or base camp. This is where people live and work and
76	set off on field trips. Some team members construct the
85	camp's buildings.
87	
	People can reach the camp by air. Pilots fly planes
97	and helicopters. They transport people and equipment
104	to the camp.

Copyright © The McGraw-Hill Companies, Inc.

Name _____

A plane flies team members home from the camp.

107   Scientists work as part of the team to learn more
117 about the Antarctic. Each scientist conducts a different
125 project. Some study the animal and plant life. Some
134 study the climate and weather. Some study the glaciers.

143   Other team members take care of buildings and
151 vehicles. Some people inspect the camp's electricity
158 system to make sure it is working. Some people fix
168 broken equipment.

170   A doctor and a nurse take care of sick team members.
181 There are firefighters who work to prevent fires.

189   Exploring the Antarctic is not a job for one person.
199 A whole team must be involved. And each team
208 member must do the job he or she knows best.

Courtesy of Keith Vanderlinde/National Science Foundation

Copyright © The McGraw-Hill Companies, Inc.

Name _____

A. Reread the passage and answer the questions.

I. What was one key detail from the passage?

_____

_____

2. What was another key detail from the passage?

_____

_____

3. What is the main idea of the passage?

_____

_____

B. Work with a partner. Read the passage aloud. Pay attention to how you pronounce the words. Stop after one minute. Fill out the chart.

	Words Read	–	Number of Errors	=	Words Correct Score
First Read		–		=	
Second Read		–		=	

Copyright © The McGraw-Hill Companies, Inc.

Name _____

Read the selection. Complete the Main Idea and Key Details chart.

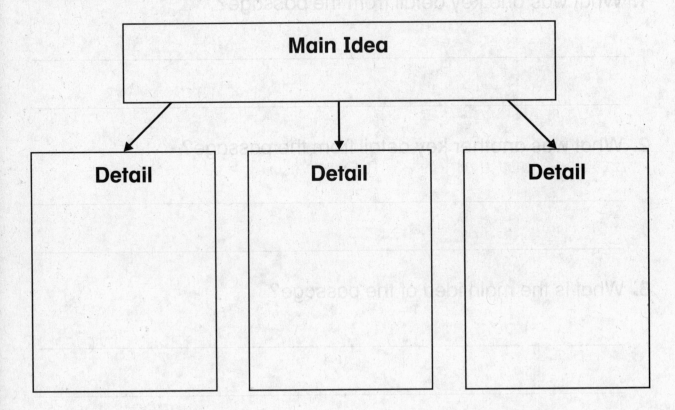

Copyright © The McGraw-Hill Companies, Inc.

Name _____

A. Read the draft model. Use the questions that follow the draft to help you think about details you can add to support the main idea.

Draft Model

Teamwork is important for jungle explorers. There are many different jobs for team members. One team member reads maps so that the other team members know where they are.

I. Why does the team need maps?

2. What other kinds of jobs might team members have?

3. What other details can you add to show why teamwork is important?

B. Now revise the draft by adding details that support and explain the main idea of teamwork.

_____

_____

_____

_____

_____

_____

Copyright © The McGraw-Hill Companies, Inc.

Name _____

A Baby Mammoth

A reindeer herder in Russia found a baby mammoth's body. She was moved to a museum. Scientists from around the world studied the baby. She was sent to Japan for tests. Scientists tried to learn all they could.

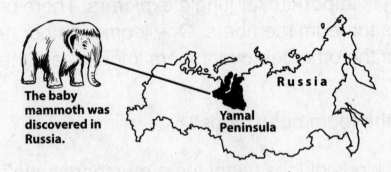

The baby mammoth was discovered in Russia.

R u s s i a

Yamal Peninsula

Answer the questions about the text.

1. How do you know this is expository text?

_____

_____

2. How did people work as a team when the baby mammoth was discovered?

_____

_____

3. What information can you learn from the map?

_____

_____

Copyright © The McGraw-Hill Companies, Inc.

Name _____

> You can figure out the meaning of unfamiliar words by looking for **word roots**. Some English words have Greek or Latin roots.
>
> | | |
> |---|---|
> | cred = to believe | spect = to look |
> | duc = to lead | sta = to stand |
> | port = to carry | struct = to build |

Read each sentence. Circle the word root in each bold print word. Then write a definition for the word.

1. The Antarctic is an **incredible** place to explore.

_____

2. One of the first jobs is to set up a research **station**, or base camp.

_____

3. Some team members **construct** the camp's buildings.

_____

4. They **transport** people and equipment to the camp.

_____

5. Some people **inspect** the camp's electricity system to make sure it is working.

_____

Copyright © The McGraw-Hill Companies, Inc.

Name _____

**Reread "An Antarctic Team." Write your opinion about
how the author used details to support the main idea of the
text. Use the words and picture to help you complete the
sentences below.**

I. The author wrote this text to tell about _____

_____

_____

2. I think the most important details are _____

_____

and _____

_____

3. These details are important because _____

_____

_____

Copyright © The McGraw-Hill Companies, Inc.

Name _____

invented	money	prices	purchase
record	system	value	worth

A. Choose the word that makes sense for each clue. Write the word on the line.

1. how much something is worth _____

2. facts that are written down about something _____

3. made something that was not around before _____

4. how much you have to pay to buy things _____

5. a plan or set of rules for doing something _____

6. the value of something _____

7. the dollars and cents you can use to buy things _____

8. to get something by paying money _____

B. Choose one vocabulary word from the box above. Write the word in a sentence of your own.

9. _____

_____

_____

Copyright © The McGraw-Hill Companies, Inc.

Name _____

> Vowel teams such as *ai*, *ay*, *oa*, *ow*, *oi*, *oy*, *oo*, and *ew* can help you read longer words with more than one syllable.

A. Read each word. Write the word from the box that has the same vowel team. Circle the letters in the vowel team.

raisin	vowel	soapy	cocoon

1. toaster _____

2. powder _____

3. sooner _____

4. contain _____

> The ending *-er* is added to an adjective to compare two nouns. The ending *-est* is added to an adjective to compare more than two nouns. Make these spelling changes before adding an ending:
> • words ending in *y*: change *y* to *i*
> • words with final *e*: drop the final *e*
> • words ending with a vowel and a consonant: double the final consonant

B. Add *-er* and *-est* to each word. Write the new words.

1. big _____ _____

2. slim _____ _____

3. windy _____ _____

Copyright © The McGraw-Hill Companies, Inc.

Name _____

Read the passage. Use the summarize strategy to tell the important ideas in your own words.

Make a Budget

You get some money, but you spend it all and have
11 nothing left. What can you do to take control? You can
22 make a budget to manage your money.

What Is a Budget?
33   A budget is a plan to keep track of money coming in
45 and money going out. The government has a budget.
54 Many families have a budget. You can have a budget,
64 too.

Income
66   First, think about money you get. Where does the
75 money come from? You might get an allowance, you
84 might earn money from a job, or you might get money
95 as a gift. All the money you get is called income.

Expenses
107   Now think about money you need to spend. Where
116 does the money go? You might have to buy lunch or pay
128 for music class. The money you spend is called expenses.

Copyright © The McGraw-Hill Companies, Inc.

Name _____

138 **Spending Money**

140   Subtract the expenses from the income. The amount
148 that is left is money you can spend on things you want.
160 You may not have enough money to buy an item you
171 want, though.

173   Here's what you can do. Set a savings goal for the
184 item. Each time you get money, set aside a portion, or
195 part, of it. You might have to save for a few weeks or a
209 few months, depending on the cost of your item. Keep
219 saving until you reach your goal. Then you can buy
229 your item.

231   Many people make a budget to manage their money.
240 You can make a budget to make your money work for
251 you. A budget will help you pay your expenses and
261 save money to buy things you want.

Copyright © The McGraw-Hill Companies, Inc.

A. Reread the passage and answer the questions.

1. What problem was described in the first paragraph of the passage?

_____

_____

2. What was one step to solving the problem?

_____

_____

3. What was the solution to the problem?

_____

_____

B. Work with a partner. Read the passage aloud. Pay attention to how you use intonation. Stop after one minute. Fill out the chart.

	Words Read	–	Number of Errors	=	Words Correct Score
First Read		–		=	
Second Read		–		=	

Copyright © The McGraw-Hill Companies, Inc.

Name _____

Read the selection. Complete the Problem and Solution chart.

```
┌─────────────────────────────────────────────────┐
│                    Problem                       │
│                                                  │
│                                                  │
└─────────────────────────────────────────────────┘
                         │
                         ▼
┌─────────────────────────────────────────────────┐
│                Steps to Solution                 │
│                                                  │
│                                                  │
│                                                  │
│                                                  │
│                                                  │
│                                                  │
└─────────────────────────────────────────────────┘
                         │
                         ▼
┌─────────────────────────────────────────────────┐
│                   Solution                       │
│                                                  │
│                                                  │
└─────────────────────────────────────────────────┘
```

Copyright © The McGraw-Hill Companies, Inc.

Name _____

A. Read the draft model. Use the questions that follow the draft to help you think about a strong conclusion you can add.

> ### Draft Model
>
> People can save money at a bank. They can get money from the bank's ATM. People also use banks for paying their bills.

I. What is the topic of the writing?

2. What is the main idea?

3. What information could you include in a conclusion sentence?

B. Now revise the draft by writing a strong conclusion that sums up the main idea.

_____

_____

_____

_____

_____

_____

Copyright © The McGraw-Hill Companies, Inc.

Name _____

How We Pay

Money Now

To pay for things now, people use bills and coins.
That may change.

Future Money

There may be no bills or
coins. People may pay
using only a computer
or a cell phone.

Answer the questions about the text.

I. How do you know this is expository text?

_____

_____

2. What is the first section of text about?

_____

_____

3. What does the subheading tell you about the second section
of text?

_____

_____

Copyright © The McGraw-Hill Companies, Inc.

Name _____

> Look at this example of **context clues** in a paragraph. The underlined words help explain what *subtract* means.
>
> **Subtract** the expenses from the income. <u>The amount that is left</u> is money you can spend on things you want.

Read each paragraph. Write the meaning of the word in bold print. Underline the context clues that helped you.

1. You get some money, but you spend it all and have nothing left. What can you do to take control? You can make a budget to **manage** your money.

   _____

2. A **budget** is a plan to keep track of money coming in and money going out. The government has a budget. Many families have a budget. You can have a budget, too.

   _____

3. First, think about money you get. Where does the money come from? You might get an allowance, you might earn money from a job, or you might get money as a gift. All the money you get is called **income**.

   _____

4. Now think about money you need to spend. Where does the money go? You might have to buy lunch or pay for music class. The money you spend is called **expenses**.

   _____

Copyright © The McGraw-Hill Companies, Inc.

Name _____

Reread "Make a Budget." Think about how the author used details and text features to write an expository text.

I. This story is an expository text because the author wrote about

_____

_____.

2. The author used the bold heading "Income" to explain to readers

_____

_____

_____.

3. The author used the bold heading "Expenses" to explain to readers

_____

_____

_____.

Copyright © The McGraw-Hill Companies, Inc.

Name _____

| create   dazzling   imagination   seconds |

A. Choose the word that makes sense for each clue. Write the word on the line.

1. something that is very bright _____

2. to make or invent something _____

3. the small parts of a minute _____

4. the ability to form ideas in your mind _____

B. Complete each sentence with a word from the box above.

5. How fast can you run in sixty _____?

6. The _____ sun was so bright it hurt my eyes.

7. Use your _____ to write a story.

8. My sister likes to _____ new kinds of cookies in the kitchen.

C. Choose one vocabulary word from the box above. Write the word in a sentence of your own.

9. _____

Copyright © The McGraw-Hill Companies, Inc.

Name _____

> When a vowel or a pair of vowels is followed by the letter *r*, it changes the vowel sound. The vowels and the *r* stay in the same syllable.

A. Read the sentences. Circle two words in each sentence that have an *r*-controlled syllable. Write each word and divide it into syllables.

1. This morning is perfect for walking in the meadow.

   _____

2. The artist paints a portrait at his easel.

   _____

3. The farmer grows garlic to sell to people.

   _____

> When you divide a longer word into syllables, each syllable must have a vowel sound.

B. Read each word. Draw a line between each syllable.

4. important   5. respectful

6. operator   7. afternoon

Copyright © The McGraw-Hill Companies, Inc.

Name _____

Read the poem. Use the summarize strategy to retell the poem in your own words.

Growing Up in One Day

If I could grow up in just one day,
09 how would I work to get my pay?
17 I could be a teacher
22 in a class,
25 helping children
27 to learn and pass.
31 The moving children
34 would be an army of ants,
40 walking to class in
44 a happy trance.

47 I could be a chef
52 in a busy kitchen,
56 I'd have helpers
59 that would always pitch in.
64 If a diner's stomach
68 was a bottomless pit,
72 My cooks and I
76 would never sit.

Copyright © The McGraw-Hill Companies, Inc.

Name _____

79	I could be a firefighter
84	in a truck,
87	putting out fires
90	and helping cats that are stuck.
96	My legs would be machines.
101	I'd climb so fast
105	and bring the cat down
110	safe at last.
113	I won't grow up
117	for quite awhile,
120	but I have some ideas
125	that make me smile.

Copyright © The McGraw-Hill Companies, Inc.

Name _____

A. Reread the passage and answer the questions.

1. How does the boy feel about being a teacher when he grows up?

_____

_____

2. How does the boy feel about being a firefighter when he grows up?

_____

_____

3. What is the boy's point of view in the poem?

_____

_____

B. Work with a partner. Read the passage aloud. Pay attention to how you use your voice to show feelings. Stop after one minute. Fill out the chart.

	Words Read	−	Number of Errors	=	Words Correct Score
First Read		−		=	
Second Read		−		=	

Copyright © The McGraw-Hill Companies, Inc.

Name _____

Read the selection. Complete the Point of View chart.

Character	Clue	Point of View

Copyright © The McGraw-Hill Companies, Inc.

Name _____

A. Read the draft model. Use the questions that follow the draft to help you think about how to make the writing better by using strong words.

Draft Model

I paint the adventures in my mind.
I make pictures of every kind.

---

1. Where could you add strong adjectives?

2. Where could you add strong adverbs?

3. Which words could you replace with stronger words?

B. Now revise the draft by adding strong words.

_____

_____

_____

_____

_____

_____

Copyright © The McGraw-Hill Companies, Inc.

Name _____

My Imagination

I dive with a whale deep into the sea,

I climb with a monkey up a tall tree.

I fly with an eagle and off we zoom,

I have lots of adventures

Without leaving my room.

Answer the questions about the text.

1. How do you know this text is a poem?

_____

_____

2. Which words at the end of lines rhyme?

_____

3. What do rhyming words add to the poem?

_____

_____

Copyright © The McGraw-Hill Companies, Inc.

> A **metaphor** compares two different things, but it does not use the word *like* or *as*.

Read the lines. Write the two things the author compares. Then explain what each metaphor means.

1. The children were an army of ants, walking to class in a happy trance.

   What two things are compared? _____

   Both things _____.

2. My legs were a machine, moving me to the finish line.

   What two things are compared? _____

   Both things _____.

3. His smile was sunlight that lit up the room.

   What two things are compared? _____

   Both things _____.

4. The runner was lightning in the race.

   What two things are compared? _____

   Both things _____.

Copyright © The McGraw-Hill Companies, Inc.

Name _____

Reread "Growing Up in One Day." Complete the sentences by writing your opinion about the poet's word choices. Use text evidence to support your opinion.

I. In the poem, the author uses words such as _____

_____

to help me understand _____

_____ .

2. I like the words _____

because they help me imagine _____

_____ .

3. I think the poet does a good job of expressing how he or she

feels about _____

because _____

_____ .

Copyright © The McGraw-Hill Companies, Inc.